THE NUT

Brigid Allen was born and brought up in the West Country. She studied History at Oxford and has worked as an archivist, manuscript cataloguer and scholarly editor in London and New York. Her books include two collections of original recipes, *Cooking with Garlic, Ginger and Chillies* (1992) and *The Soup Book* (Macmillan, 1993); a history of Oxford's oldest family-owned business, *Morrells of Oxford: the Family and their Brewery, 1743–1993* (1994); and the literary and historical *Food: an Oxford Anthology* (1994). She lives in a small Cotswold town with her husband and son.

by the same author

THE SOUP BOOK

BRIGID ALLEN

The NUT BOOK

M

MACMILLAN

LONDON

First published 1994 by Macmillan London Limited

a division of Pan Macmillan Publishers Limited
Cavaye Place London SW10 9PG
and Basingstoke

Associated companies throughout the world

ISBN 0-333-60635-3

1 3 5 7 9 8 6 4 2

A CIP catalogue record for this book is available from
the British Library

Illustrated by Nicky Adam

Typeset by CentraCet Limited, Cambridge
Printed by Mackays of Chtham plc

CONTENTS

Acknowledgements

Data from *Fruit and Nuts* on pp. 11–13 are reproduced with the permission of the Royal Society of Chemistry and the Controller of Her Majesty's Stationery Office.

The Syndicat d'Initiative, Montélimar, provided me promptly with free information about nougat. I owe thanks to my editor, Judith Hannam, for her patience and encouragement, and to members of my family for graciously adapting to nuts with everything. I wish to thank especially two restaurateurs, Ethel Ow of Munchy Munchy, Park End Street, Oxford, and Alberto Portugheis of Rhapsody, Richmond Way, London W14, for kindly allowing me to reproduce several of their recipes.

Weights and Measures

THE METRIC equivalents given to imperial weights and measures in this book are consistent but necessarily approximate. (1 oz = 28.31 g, not 25 g. Again, 10 fl oz / ½ pint = 283.1 ml, not 300 ml).

As a member of a generation brought up to imperial weights and measures, I continue to cook using these, and translate into metric when necessary. Anyone curious to know the actual measurements which I used when concocting my own original recipes for this book would be advised to consult the imperial figures given, not their metric equivalents.

At the same time I am disinclined to encourage too much rigidity in weighing amd measuring, when excesses (or their opposites) of one ingredient or another can usually be balanced out by adjusting the rest. Why dirty the scales with a lump of butter, or fiddle around enclosing this in clingfilm before weighing it, when your eye can tell you roughly how to divide a 250 g block of it? Why search out the 300-ml mark on a metric measuring-jug (or, if scrupulously accurate, find this, then subtract just over 15 ml), when you can half-fill a pint-sized milk bottle to arrive at 10 fl oz? No doubt the abolition of doorstep milk deliveries will eventually make this kind of domestic subversion difficult. Meanwhile, however, I should like to point out, for those who find the concepts of 300 ml and 10 fl oz as vague as I do, that the following rough equivalents apply:

142/150 ml = 5 fl oz = ¼ pint
190/200 ml = 6.5/7 fl oz = ⅓ pint
284/300 ml = 10 fl oz = ½ pint
380/400 ml = 13/14 fl oz = ⅔ pint
426/450 ml = 15 fl oz – ¾ pint

INTRODUCTION

E ATING NUTS, a timelessly ancient human stratagem for sur-
vival, is also one which unites the most diverse parts of the
world. From the pistachio and pine nut cultures of the eastern
Mediterranean countries to the commercialized peanut-butter and
jelly culture of North America; from China to East and West
Africa and Brazil; and from the hazelnuts, chestnuts, and cultivated walnuts of northern Europe to the macadamia nut and
cashew plantations of South-East Asia, southern India and northern Australia, nut-eating, or at least nut-gathering and exporting,
creates an invisible web. Vegetarians eat nuts, as do meat-eaters;
rice, millet, cassava, maize, potato, oat, and wheat-eaters eat nuts;
large-scale chocolate-consumers eat quantities of them, as do
people who eat no chocolate or sweets of any kind. At the same
time, nut-eating is a generally marginal activity, and in the West
can be regarded as eccentric. Accepted as a snack, or as an
ingredient of cakes or component of the traditional after-dinner
dessert, nuts can be condemned or ridiculed as crank food when
substituted for meat, as they have been by many Western vegetarians during the past hundred years.

The arrangement in the southern English supermarket where
I shop reflects some of this ambivalence. On the cake-ingredients
shelf are small packets, rarely weighing more than 100 g/3½ oz, of
'Continental style' roasted ground hazelnuts, slivered almonds,
and 'natural' shelled almonds, hazelnuts, walnuts, pecans. One
aisle over, with the savoury snacks for nibbling with drinks, are
pistachios, peanuts, and small bags of the same nuts as those on
the cake-making counter, all roasted and with more or less copious
additions of salt. On the fruit counter are the unshelled nuts –
Californian walnuts, pecans, and chestnuts or hazelnuts in season.
A new addition to this last display is a collection of small, 80–100 g
plastic vacuum packs of the more exotic nuts ready shelled –

macadamia nuts from Australia, pine nuts from China, and sweet-tasting Roman hazelnuts from Italy. Nut-eating is clearly on the increase as far as this supermarket chain is concerned; although whether it is assumed to take place seriously, in the context of formal meals, or merely as a healthy or appetite-dulling drink-stimulating snack, is yet to be revealed.

In the past, different types of nut have meant different things depending on their consumers' nationality, region, or socio-economic group. In England and the rest of northern Europe, from the late Middle Ages onwards, the use of almonds in cooking was seen as a sign of dignity, luxury, and wealth. Imported almonds were expensive and, when blanched and ground, gave sweet soups and brawn or chicken dishes a prized white colour and an incomparable delicacy of texture and taste. Some countries, notably France, took their devotion to almonds further and developed a classic, almond-based *pâtisserie*, diversifying in Provence into honey-based nougat. In nineteenth-century England, however, with its acceptance of substitute and imitation foods, its combination of gastronomic wastefulness and parsimony, and its determination to relegate all cooking to a hired chef or ill-paid female servants, almonds ceased to be regarded as the superfine material with which ladies produced the special delicacies of kitchen and still-room, and all but disappeared in cake-making in favour of flour and artificial flavouring.

Hazelnuts were hedge-food in Britain, but material for elaborate cakes in Poland and Hungary and for sauces and soups in Spain. Walnuts were gathered green in England for pickling, or left to mature and dry out to crack open and nibble plain for dessert. In France, on the other hand, vine- and nut-growers enjoyed freshly ripened walnuts as a relish with salt and new wine; and from Spain across France to central Europe, dried chopped or pounded walnuts appeared in a variety of regional biscuits and cakes. Chestnuts were the food of the poor in mountainous regions such as the Apennines or the Massif Central, where they served as a cheap, stodgy, not particularly nutritious replacement for bread. Rich Italians in the seventeenth century perfumed them with rose-water and ate them as sweets, while sophisticated French cooks perfected the art of creating *marrons glacés* and *Mont Blanc*. The British, characteristically, preferred to eat their chestnuts plain, roasted in the ashes of open fires as a rustic, seasonal treat.

Some people detest nuts; others find in them a source of satisfaction for their deepest nutritional cravings. While the British abandoned the art of cooking and confecting generously with nuts, and came to regard such Continental treats as *pralines*, *turrón*, or *Gâteau de Pithiviers* with the respect due to the unattainably exotic, they still indulged in seasonal nut-eating, from autumnal chestnut-roasting and chestnut-based stuffing for turkeys to the bowlfuls of miscellaneous unshelled nuts which gather dust and dross on many sideboards and kitchen dressers in the months after Christmas. The traditional British Christmas or wedding cake is still covered, under its ceremonial hard white icing, with a layer of yellow-dyed or putty-coloured marzipan, in token deference to the love of almond confectionery which once united us with our Continental neighbours.

There are times, too, when people seem content to eat food which ostensibly contains a high proportion of real nuts, but the manufacturers of which are effectively deceiving them with cheaper substitutes. The 'almond' macaroons sold in most British bakers' shops and supermarkets, heavily sweetened, artificially flavoured, darkened with caramel colouring, and decorated on top with a single flake of slivered almond, are clearly not made only, if indeed at all, from the traditional ingredients of beaten egg white, ground almonds, and sugar. Temptingly packeted factory-made 'frangi-pani cakes', of supposedly Belgian origin, consist mainly of sugar, flour, colouring, and almond flavouring. Nutty breakfast cereals such as cornflakes prove, on tasting, to contain a high proportion of sugar and a minimal one of nuts, 'almond' crunchy cereals to be artifically flavoured, and mixed nut cereals such as muesli to be based very largely on coarse-tasting peanuts.

Yet we can eat nuts, in whatever quantities we like, undisguised by sugar or synthetic flavourings, and without reference to the meanness of the food manufacturing industry. Health-food shops such as Neal's Yard in London and the Home Counties sell ready-shelled nuts by the 250 g, 500 g, and even (for plain, unroasted peanuts) 1 kg bags. In oriental food shops you can sometimes buy a 3 kg bag of ready-shelled almonds, probably intended for the restaurant trade. The bigger the quantity bought, the less, proportionately, the nuts cost; and the joy of possessing 3 kg of almonds (with all their potential for biscuits, cakes, soups, curries, vegetable dishes, breakfast cereal, and ice-cream) is all the greater for considering the cost of the equivalent amount in 100 g bags.

Many of the nuts which we now take for granted – cashews, macadamia nuts, pecans, pine nuts, pistachios – are relatively recent imports from America, China, India, or Australia. Others, such as Brazil nuts and coconuts, reflect long-established trading relationships between various tropical countries and Britain. Peanuts, with their almost exclusively American origin, have been around in increasingly large quantities since soon after the end of the Second World War: at first roasted and salted or plain and mixed with raisins; latterly, in addition, dry-roasted and sometimes harshly flavoured, or as an ingredient in breakfast cereals and chocolate bars. (Known as groundnuts, they featured in a British political disaster of the late 1940s, when massive investment by the Labour government in a groundnut oil scheme for Africa went hopelessly wrong.)

The most traditionally familiar nuts in Britain are almonds, chestnuts, hazelnuts, and walnuts. Either gathered in Britain or imported from Continental countries (when Californian almonds had not yet flooded the European market), they survived the commercial blockades of the two world wars, and were seasonally available as an important source of protein when meat was rationed. Late Victorian and Edwardian vegetarians had been only half aware of protein, and doggedly ate chestnuts in the hope that these would replace the protein lost to them in meat, fish, and eggs.

By the late 1930s, on the other hand, the foundations had been laid for much of our present knowledge of nutrition. When rationing came into force in 1939, common sense pointed country-dwellers in the direction of the hedges and fields, to gather rosehips and green walnuts for Vitamin C and ripe walnuts or hazelnuts for protein. In the early years of the war Claire Loewenfeld, a writer living at Tring in Hertfordshire, issued a series of pamphlets entitled *Britain's Wild Larder*, urging the use of all such nuts and berries, and anticipating by thirty years the self-sufficiency manuals of the wholefood era such as Richard Mabey's *Food For Free* (1972). 'An abundant variety can be taken from the shelves of the wild larder,' she wrote bracingly. 'Old clothes, gloves, scissors, Wellingtons, a crooked walking stick to get the bushes down, and a basket, are all the instruments we need.'

After the war, Claire Loewenfeld developed her pamphlets into two books, on mushrooms and nuts, published as the *Britain's Wild Larder* series by Faber & Faber in 1956 and 1957. *Nuts*, the second of these books, beautifully illustrated with wood-engravings, is classically evocative of the now unpopular period of post-war rationing, gastronomic insularity, and earnest-minded frugality in the kitchen. Concentrating on recipes for almonds, chestnuts, hazelnuts, and walnuts, it is a repository of foods which were going out of fashion as the book was published: cheese and nut balls, nut creams, mayonnaise and nut sandwiches, green walnut jam or marmalade, and grated or milled nuts as an accompaniment to that important wartime feature, the 'daily raw salad'. Some of the recipes are central European in origin, like Swiss Chestnut Soup or Austrian Steamed Walnut Pudding; and all are bland enough to have belonged to the canon of pre-war international vegetarianism. Three additional sections cover beechmast, acorns, and horse chestnuts: the first two as human food or the basis of ersatz coffee, the last as animal fodder.

The most endearing aspect of *Nuts* is perhaps its background information, which includes copious quotations from John Evelyn's *Sylva*, historical and botanical details about almond, chestnut, hazelnut, and walnut trees, and nutritional comparisons between nuts and other foods (reminding us, for example, that unripe walnuts contain more Vitamin C than rosehips, two Brazil nuts contain as much energy value as an ounce of beef or cheese, and hazelnuts contain one and a half times as much protein as the

equivalent weight in eggs). Although the book contains no reference to saturated and unsaturated fats, the subject of many of our
present-day nutritional preoccupations, it includes tables (dated
1937) showing the different food values of nuts in terms of protein,
fat, carbohydrates, calcium, phosphorus, iron, and calories or
energy. It also reminds us of the importance of many nuts as good
acid-free sources of calcium and phosphorus, since most nuts (with
the exception of walnuts) deposit a harmlessly alkaline residue in
the body when their organic matter is burnt up during digestion,
whereas most other proteinous foods containing phosphorus are
acid-forming.

In an age of instant gastronomic eclecticism, with fresh, dried,
or vacuum-packed tropical nuts, fruits, and other produce constantly available to those who can afford them, Claire Loewenfeld's
frugal message is still clear. Over fifty years after the appearance
of her wartime pamphlets, eating nuts remains one of the ecologi-
cally least wasteful forms of human nourishment. Cultivated nuts
(to which Claire Loewenfeld devoted a large part of her book,
alongside the hazelnuts, beechmast, and acorns of the wild larder)
can in most cases be grown on quite poor soil without requiring
huge amounts of artificial fertilizer; are relatively simple, cheap,
and hygienic to package, and often remain sealed in their shells
from tree to consumer. They do not attract additives or colouring
agents (unless transformed into a factory product such as almond
marzipan), and give rise to a valuable by-product for joinery and
manufacturing, the wood of spent trees. If nuts are culled from the
wild, this upsets the balance of nature only by removing a tiny
fraction of the winter food of squirrels.

Nutritionally, meanwhile, nuts, seeds, and their oils have
become acclaimed by medical and dietary researchers as key items
in the ideal diet for the more urbanized and industrialized parts of
the world. Most nut oils are high in mono-unsaturated or polyunsaturated fats, which are now recognized to be safer than saturated
fats in a diet aimed at reducing the likelihood of coronary heart
disease. Many nuts also contain significant amounts of Vitamin E,
an important factor in reducing the risk of heart disease and

possibly also of cancer. Calcium, found in nuts without the accompanying saturated fat content found in unskimmed milk and cheese, is essential for the growth and continued strengthening of teeth and bones in young and old. Potassium, which occurs in generous quantities in certain nuts (426 mg per 55 g of total food content in almonds; 400 mg per 55 g in peanuts), is a valuable preventative against strokes.

Mono-unsaturated and Polyunsaturated Fatty Acids

Advertisements for polyunsaturated oils began to appear in the United States in the 1960s, when the national diet, especially among the non-hippie young, was high in saturated fats from lavish quantities of ice cream, full-cream milk shakes, hamburgers, steaks, and french fries. Heart attacks had already been identified as a major cause of premature death, especially among younger middle-aged men. These were generally blamed, however, as much on stress at work and on the effects of a largely sedentary office and home life as on the national cholesterol-rich diet. It was only after autopsies were carried out on selected casualties of the Vietnam War, well-nourished young American conscripts with strong bones, long limbs, and perfect teeth, revealing that many of them already showed premature hardening of the arteries caused by habitually eating and drinking foods high in saturated fat, that the virtues of American-style meat and dairy products began to seem tarnished. In Britain, awareness of the probable effects of a diet high in saturated fat took even longer to percolate through to the general public, who in the 1960s were still recovering from the austerities of poverty and rationing, and were half-guiltily spooning cream over their pudding in the knowledge that to do so was extravagant and might make them spotty or fat, but with no thought of any longer-term repercussions on their systems.

Similarly, the concept of 'protective foods' containing polyunsaturated fatty acids (PUFAs), which help to inhibit the clotting effects of saturated fats, has been only gradually accepted in Britain. Nutritionists point out that PUFAs can be found not only in many oils and non-hydrogenated margarines but in nuts, seeds, oily fish, and root and leaf vegetables. Advertising, however, continues to distract attention from this point by merely emphasizing the absence of saturated fats from various 'lite' dairy or mock-dairy products, and ignoring the nuts, seeds, fish, and vegetables which the advertiser has not been briefed to promote. In the mean time, the British recession of the late 1980s and early 1990s has if anything produced a reaction against austerity in cooking, with a proliferation of books and television cookery programmes exploring the delights of lavish cakes and desserts rich in chocolate and whipped cream.

Most nuts contain a higher proportion of mono-unsaturated than polyunsaturated fat. Mono-unsaturated fats, such as the fat predominant in olive oil, used to be explained as neither damaging the arteries nor positively tending to protect them against the ill effects of saturated fats. Recently, however, it has been discovered that the oleic acid found in mono-unsaturated fats is an anti-oxidant, helping to prevent the process of lipid peroxidation by damaging, elusive agents known as free radicals, which can enter the body through cigarette smoke or other forms of poison. Once free radicals succeed in peroxidating lipids (otherwise cholesterol molecules), they can turn these rancid or toxic and cause them to mass together in cells which then clot against the artery walls. The presence of cholesterol in the body is not, therefore, automatically harmful in itself, provided that the system takes in enough antioxidants to maintain a constant protection against assaults by free radicals.

Antioxidants and Vitamin E

Some nuts and seeds contain a high proportion of Vitamin E. Not all books agree about the precise amounts which are present in certain foods. The fifth supplement to McCance and Widdowson's *Composition of Foods* (1992), quoted in the tables on pp. 11–13, gives the following amounts of Vitamin E per type of nut or seed, in mg per 100 g: sunflower seeds, 37.77; hazelnuts, 24.98; almonds, 23.96;

Brazil nuts, 7.18; pecans, 4.34; walnuts, 3.85; dry-roasted peanuts, 1.11; cashews, 0.85; roasted, salted peanuts, 0.66. An American health-food cookery book, published only in the previous year, gives an almost completely different set of figures for Vitamin E content in mg per 100 g: sunflower seeds, 52; hazelnuts, 21; almonds, 21; Brazil nuts, 7; pecans, 2; walnuts, 22; roasted peanuts, 11; cashews, 11. It is important to remember, therefore, that not every cookery book can be considered an infallible authority, and that many figures given in such books may be approximate.

Vitamin E is present in small quantities in many foods, and is important as an antioxidant once free radicals have caused cholesterol molecules to coagulate in the membrane of fatty cells in the blood. Vitamin C, also an antioxidant, is effective only in the watery part of the blood, whereas Vitamin E is fat-soluble and effective in the fatty part. A high intake of Vitamin E through nuts and seeds is thus important as another means of protection against lipid peroxidation in the blood.

Keeping and Grinding Nuts

Nuts are best stored in their shells, unless the effort of cracking them means that you avoid eating them at all. Californian walnuts, peanuts, and pistachios (these two last often sold roasted but unhulled) are all easy to shell. Almonds are difficult, but keep reasonably well out of the shell and are now almost invariably sold ready-shelled. Once shelled, nuts are best stored away from the light in airtight containers.

Some nuts, especially pine nuts, are soft and oily enough to grind with a pestle and mortar. For others, use the coffee-grinding attachment of a liquidizer. Most nuts can be ground and used unblanched unless you want a particularly delicate, pale effect.

The Recipes

Initially, when I planned this book, I intended to go abroad in search of recipes for nuts. Many of my impressions of travel and living abroad have been bound up (I realized in retrospect) with buying and eating nuts or nutty treats. In New York there were the pleasures of pecan pie and butter pecan ice cream; the smouldering braziers of chestnuts near Grand Central Station; and the little nut shop on the Upper West Side from which a paper cone of shelled, mixed nuts would fuel the long, exhilarating walk downtown on a bright, cold Saturday morning in autumn. From a similar shop, I believe in Utrecht, I still have an elegant little purpose-made nut bag with a pattern of hazelnuts. In Italy, over thirty years ago, there was the discovery of brilliantly vivid pistachio ice cream, and delicious little almond biscuits, bought furtively to fill the aching void between a cup of tea or coffee for breakfast and the working family's late pasta lunch. Travelling on buses and trains in India, I lived largely on bags of cashews and on the standard vegetarian food of cheap restaurants and station buffets; but a rare treat was a dish of Mughlai chicken, scattered in the Persian tradition with roasted, slivered almonds and edged with silver leaf.

In the end, however, most of the recipes here are non-traditional and my own. Sources of inspiration have included Lesley Chamberlain's *Food and Cooking of Eastern Europe* (1989), a cookery and travel book written before the present tragedy of ethnic civil war in south-eastern Europe; the chapter devoted to recipes for walnuts in Jane Grigson's *Good Things* (1973); Hilary Spurling's imaginative edition of *Elinor Fettiplace's Receipt Book* (1986), with its many sixteenth- and early seventeenth-century almond recipes; and the Neal's Yard Wholefood Warehouse in Covent Garden, London, Oxford, and elsewhere, an unfailing source of good, varied, generously packed nuts and seeds.

Protein and Fat Content of Nuts and Seeds (g per 100 g)

	Protein		Fat
Peanuts (plain)	25.6	Macadamia nuts (salted)	77.6
Peanuts (dry roasted)	25.5	Pecans	70.1
Almonds	21.1	Coconut (creamed)	68.8
Cashews (roast, salted)	20.5	Pine nuts	68.6
Sunflower seeds	19.8	Walnuts	68.5
Tahini (sesame) paste	18.5	Brazil nuts	68.2
Sesame seeds	18.2	Hazelnuts	63.5
Pistachios (roast, salted)	17.9	Tahini (sesame) paste	58.9
Cashews (plain)	17.7	Sesame seeds	58.0
Walnuts	14.7	Almonds	55.8
Hazelnuts	14.1	Pistachios (roast, salted)	55.4
Brazil nuts	14.1	Peanuts (roast, salted)	53.0
Pine nuts	14.0	Cashews (roast, salted)	50.9
Pecans	9.2	Cashews (plain)	48.2
Macadamia nuts	7.9	Sunflower seeds	47.5
Coconut (creamed)	6.0	Peanuts (plain)	46.1
Coconut (desiccated)	5.6	Coconut (fresh)	36.0
Coconut (fresh)	3.2	Chestnuts (dried)	5.1
Chestnuts (fresh)	2.0	Chestnuts (fresh)	2.7

(From B. Holland, I. D. Unwin and D. H. Buss, *Fruit and Nuts*. The first supplement to McCance and Widdowson's *The Composition of Foods* (5th edition), Royal Society of Chemistry, 1992, 88–92.) All figures refer to shelled or husked nuts and seeds.

Fat Fractions of Nuts and Seeds (g per 100 g)

	Polyunsaturated	Mono-unsaturated	Saturated
Macadamia nuts (plain)	1.6	60.8	11.2
Pecans	18.7	42.5	5.7
Coconut (creamed)	1.6	3.9	59.3
Pine nuts	41.1	19.9	4.6
Walnuts	47.5	12.4	5.6
Brazil nuts	23.0	25.8	16.4
Hazelnuts	5.9	50.0	4.7
Sesame seeds	25.5	21.7	8.3
Almonds	14.2	34.4	4.7
Pistachios (roasted, salted)	17.9	27.6	7.4
Cashews (plain)	8.8	27.8	9.5
Sunflower seeds	47.5	31.0	9.8
Peanuts (plain)	14.3	21.1	8.2
Coconut (fresh)	0.8	2.0	31.0
Chestnuts (plain)	1.1	1.0	0.5

(From B. Holland, I. D. Unwin and D. H. Buss, *Fruit and Nuts*. The first supplement to McCance and Widdowson's *The Composition of Foods* (5th edition), Royal Society of Chemistry, 1992, 106.) All figures refer to shelled or husked nuts and seeds, and are fractions of the total fat content already given.

Vitamin Content of Nuts and Seeds (mg per 100 g)

	Carotene	Vitamin E	Thiamin	Riboflavin	Niacin
Almonds		23.96	0.21	0.75	3.1
Brazil nuts		7.18	0.67	0.03	0.3
Cashews (plain)	6.0	0.85	0.69	0.14	1.2
Cashews (roasted)	6.0	1.30	0.41	0.16	1.3
Chestnuts (fresh)		1.20	0.14	0.02	0.4
Coconut (fresh)		0.73	0.04	0.01	0.5
Hazelnuts		24.98	0.43	0.16	1.1
Macadamia nuts (salted)		1.49	0.28	0.06	1.6
Peanuts (plain)		10.09	1.14	0.10	13.8
Peanuts (dry roasted)		1.11	0.18	0.13	13.1
Peanuts (roast, salted)		0.66	0.18	0.10	13.6
Pecans	50.0	4.34	0.71	0.15	1.4
Pine nuts	10.0	13.65	0.73	0.19	3.8
Pistachios	130.0	4.16	0.70	0.23	1.7
Sesame seeds	6.0	2.53	0.93	0.17	5.0
Sunflower seeds	15.0	37.77	1.60	0.19	4.1
Walnuts		3.85	0.40	0.14	1.2

(From B. Holland, I. D. Unwin and D. H. Buss, *Fruit and Nuts*. The first supplement to McCance and Widdowson's *The Composition of Foods* (5th edition), Royal Society of Chemistry, 1992, 93–103.)

ALMONDS

(*Prunus amygdalus, prunus dulcis*)

I N NORTHERN Europe, almonds have long symbolized lightness, delicacy, hopefulness, and spring. Easter cakes, or confections like the Russian *paskha*, have often included or been based on almonds. In medieval cookery, almond milk or ground almonds performed the function which classic French cooks gradually transferred to cream, giving dishes of white meats, sweet soups, or sweetened curds an extra delicacy and lightness. Almonds were expensive imports, brought across the Alps from southern Europe, and were prized as rich men's food for the whiteness of the confections which contained them. At feasts, where courses of many dishes were set out on the table for guests to help themselves, these light dishes offset the great majority of gross dripping brown and red dishes such as venison, game, spit-roasted beef, and tusked boars' heads. Later, almonds became a favourite ingredient in ladies' cookery, together with the newly imported West Indian sugar, fine flour, cream, spices, sack or Malmsey, and eggs.

The almond tree, with its pink flowers appearing in January or February in Mediterranean countries and in February or March farther north, has itself always been symbolically important. In

Hebrew the word for almond means 'the early one'; and the almond was regarded as the most sacred tree in ancient Israel. In the Book of Exodus, God tells Moses to make the *menorah*, the ceremonial branched candlestick for the tabernacle, with candle-holders resembling almonds and their flowers. In the Book of Numbers, Aaron's rod shows his special status by blossoming with almond flowers and nuts. Ecclesiastes proclaims, mysteriously, that 'the almond tree shall flourish, and the grasshopper shall be a burden, and desire shall fail: because man goeth to his long home, and the mourners go about the streets'.

Amygdalum, the Latin term for almond, comes from the ancient Greek *amygdalē*, showing that the almond tree became naturalized from the eastern to the western Mediterranean. (The later Latin word *amendla* gave us the French *amande*, the German *Mandel* and the Italian *mandorla*.) Towards the end of the sixteenth century the Provençal gentleman Olivier de Serres planted almond orchards on his estate at Pradel, near Lyon, introducing the serious cultivation of the almond into France. The fashion spread rapidly northwards into England; and in 1597 John Gerard reported in his *Herball* that almond trees were grown in many gardens and orchards around London. Like the cultivation of the apricot, melon, peach, grape, and pineapple, almond-growing undoubtedly provided an irresistible challenge for British gardeners, convinced that well-tended soil and a sheltering south wall could produce success in Middlesex equal to anything in Provence. English almonds, however, have always been unreliable and small. The many almond trees growing now in little slots of town gardens, from which they jut out brightly in flower into the greyness of February and March, seem to function purely as seasonal spirit-lifters rather than providers of usable fruit.

Almonds flourish in warm, dry climates from California to Spain, and from southern Italy, Sicily, Greece, and Turkey eastwards to Iran, Afghanistan, and China. In most countries where they are grown they are treated as a sweet or savoury-sweet delicacy, contributing to saffron-coloured *polos* and *pillaus*, enriching oriental and Middle Eastern lamb, duck, fish, and chicken dishes, and appearing in sweets and desserts, from the Spanish marzipan-like *turrón* and Italian *amaretti* (made with bitter almonds) to the Chinese ceremonial almond junket, sweet almond soup, and almond cookies. Their taste and texture have dominated fine European *pâtisserie* for centuries, in *pralines*, *Gâteau de Pithiviers*, *Dacquoise*, *Linzer Torte*, and many other elaborate nut-based and nut-flavoured pastries as well as in the humbler, often over-sweetened and artificially flavoured macaroon.

In Britain, where almonds were important in the kind of enjoyable still-room cooking undertaken by ladies, a frugal tendency sometimes caused cooks to stretch their supplies of ground almonds for cake-making by overwhelming them with flour so that the taste and texture were lost. The invention of almond essence compensated for this loss by encouraging the mean-minded to banish ground almonds from cake-ingredients altogether, reserving them for the heavily sweetened marzipan icing of fruit cakes. In Jewish cooking, on the other hand, ground almonds were highly regarded as a substitute for flour on special, ritual occasions. Eliza Acton, in her *Modern Cookery . . . for Private Families* (1845), describes a (probably Sephardic) Jewish almond pudding very like the traditional Spanish and Majorcan almond cakes which are still made today. Half a pound each of almonds and sugar were mixed with ten egg yolks, seven well-beaten whites, and a little orange-flower water, and baked until just firm, before being served with a powdering of sifted sugar or a syrup flavoured with orange-flower water, noyau, or maraschino. The almonds, Eliza Acton observed, could be bought ready-ground from a 'Jew confectioner', probably in the West End of London. Noyau, the liqueur, was a popular Victorian flavouring, made by infusing brandy with fruit-kernels or a commercial substance known as almond cake.

The health-giving properties of almonds justify their world-wide popularity. They are high in protein, containing 21.1 g per 100 g of all food values. This makes them richer in protein than any kind of red meat, and only slightly less rich, weight for weight, than boneless chicken, Cheddar cheese, or peanuts (the most proteinous of all nuts, containing 25.6 g per 100 g). Like many other proteinous foods such as cheese, red meat, and walnuts, almonds are rich in the essential minerals phosphorus and calcium. Unlike these other foods, however (but like many other, less protein-rich, nuts, fruit, and vegetables), almonds leave an alkalinic rather than an acidic residue in the body's system when their organic matter has been consumed. Eating almonds therefore helps to preserve the body's acid–alkali balance, which is often upset by consuming too many acidic, high-protein foods.

Almonds are moderately rich in both mono-unsaturated and polyunsaturated fats, and very low in saturated fats. They are rich in Vitamin E, which helps protect against the oxidation of cholesterol molecules in the fatty part of the blood. (Sunflower seeds contain 37.77 mg of Vitamin E per 100 g, hazelnuts 24.98 mg, almonds 23.96 mg, and most other nuts less than 10 mg.) They are higher in biotin (Vitamin H) than any other nuts apart from peanuts.

Combining almonds with other foods, as cooks have done in medieval Europe and still do in the traditional cooking of many parts of the world today, shows an instinctive understanding of the kind of nutritional balance which brings out the best in all foods. In a chicken or beef dish with almonds, the two complementary sources of protein help to maintain the acid–alkali balance of the body. In a pilaff or cake containing almonds, the cereals present help to make available the protein in the nuts. Even handfuls of nuts eaten at odd times during the day can help to maintain this nutritional balance to the body's benefit.

Buying Almonds

Almonds are harder to crack than most other nuts, with the exception of macadamia nuts. They are in any case relatively hard to find in the shell, but can be bought in quite large quantities unblanched (a state in which they keep for much longer than when blanched) from health-food shops or oriental grocery stores. Neal's Yard Wholefood Warehouse, at Covent Garden in London, the Golden Cross in Oxford, and elsewhere, at the time of writing sells

500 g packets of shelled, unblanched Californian almonds, 25% cheaper than five of the standard 100 g packets of similar almonds available in many supermarkets.

Blanching and Grinding Almonds

Ready-blanched, ready-ground almonds bought from shops vary greatly in texture, quality, and freshness. Almonds ground at home in a blender attachment or a clean coffee grinder are cheaper than the shop-bought kind, can be deliberately ground finely or coarsely, and sometimes have a pleasant irregularity of texture. For cakes, biscuits, and macaroons I usually grind almonds unblanched, since baking diminishes the slightly bitter taste of the skins.

To blanch almonds, pour them into a bowl and cover them with boiling water. Leave them for several minutes, then drain off the water and replace it with freshly boiling water. The almonds will then pop out of their skins very easily.

Leek and Almond Soup

EXPENSIVE, time-consuming blanched almonds were a favourite form of thickening for luxury soups in England from the late Middle Ages to the early nineteenth century. John Fordham, Bishop of Durham, provided *Potage de Blandesore*, a creamy soup of almonds blended with capons' flesh, almond milk, and a red colouring, and *Potage bruet of Almondes*, a sweet cream soup made with curds, honey, almonds, and butter, at the lavish dinner of three courses and dozens of rich, meaty dishes which he gave for King Richard II at his London palace on 23 September 1387. (Six months later Fordham was translated to the bishopric of Ely, where he remained, presumably satisfied, until his death in 1425.)

The descendant of these decorative, delicious soups, 'white soup', persisted until early this century, becoming steadily down-graded as it did so from a treat to a duty. Economical Victorian cooks, keener on the number of courses composing a meal than on their quality, left out the almonds and perpetrated tastelessly nasty versions of white soup made with milk, white root vegetables, cornflour, rice, or, as my Edwardian edition of Mrs Beeton unappealingly suggests, tinned rabbit.

If you find blanching almonds as soothing and enjoyable as I do, this light creamy-yellow soup is well worth the effort and expense of making it.

SERVES 4–6

675 g/1½ lb fine leeks, cleaned and sliced
2–3 tablespoons olive oil
1 large carrot, peeled and chopped
1 teaspoon sea salt
10–12 black peppercorns, bruised in a mortar
1.25 litres/2¼ pints water, chicken stock, or stock + water
120 g/4 oz almonds, blanched and ground

Put the leeks into a large, heavy pan with the oil, cover and leave to simmer, stirring once or twice, for 20–25 minutes. After 5–10 minutes, when the leeks have begun to give off some of their liquid, add the carrot. When the vegetables have softened, add the sea salt, black peppercorns, and water or stock (modifying the seasoning if using stock which is already seasoned). Add the almonds, which are best blanched and ground at home for freshness and an interesting, slight irregularity of texture. Bring to the boil and simmer for 15–20 minutes, then cool slightly and liquidize. The almonds have a similar thickening effect to potatoes; but this soup is sweeter, creamier, and frothier than the standard leek-and-potato. Serve hot as a light supper dish with good bread and cheese, or cold for lunch.

Almond and Olive Rings

A LMONDS, light, bland, and naturally sweet, are not usually associated with dark, briny-tasting olives, except to the extent that both come from Mediterranean areas. Apart from salting almonds as a high-class snack to serve with drinks, the traditional tendency has been to regard all almonds as material for sugary biscuits, marzipan, cakes, or macaroons, while keeping olives for hors-d'œuvres and decorating slabs of pizza. I always welcome un-sweet almond dishes, however, and felt convinced that this particular combination would work. Serve these little mouthfuls with drinks, as appetizers, or at a cold summer lunch with salads, good bread, thin slices of honey-roast ham, and perhaps a light green pungently herby purée of new broad beans and cashew nuts (see page 70).

MAKES 12–16 LITTLE PASTRIES

---

120 g/4 oz whole unblanched almonds
60 g/2 oz cream cheese
100 g/3½ oz plain black olives (not pre-stoned)
1 egg yolk, for glazing

Grind the almonds, skins and all, in a blender until they are just mealy. Tip them into a mixing bowl, rub in the cream cheese, and add a teaspoon or two of cold water to make a consistent ball of not too sticky dough. Flour a board and roll out the pastry into a rough oblong, about 20 × 13 cm/8 × 5 in. Stone the olives and arrange them in halves or pieces to cover the pastry. (Stoning or pitting your own olives is not always a tidy operation; but they taste much better this way than do the rubbery, characterless ones which have been mechanically deprived of their stones before bottling or arrival in loose form in the shops.) Roll the pastry round the olives to form a sausage-roll shape and glaze all over with egg yolk. Do not worry if the pastry is stiff and tends to fall apart; a little patching will go unnoticed once the roll is cooked. Pre-heat the oven to 190°C/375°F, Gas mark 5 and bake the roll for 15–20 minutes until it is a richly glazed golden-brown. Now slice it carefully into cross-sections, each with the purplish-grey flesh of the cut-through olives enclosed in a ring of almond pastry. Arrange on a plate and serve very fresh, either warm or just cool.

Chicken with an Almond and Olive Crust

I AM FOND OF black olives as the main constituent of a crust for roasting or baking meat. Their juicy robustness gives an extra strength and colour to meat-juice, resulting in wonderfully potent gravy. A half-leg of lamb is especially good roasted with its exposed surface covered in a paste of black olives pounded up with Greek yoghurt. By the end of the cooking-time the juices from the roast will have deliciously permeated this crust, and the meat within will be tender and well-flavoured.

This recipe for chicken is lighter, but still results in a filling meal. Chicken quarters are baked in a paste made of olives and almonds, and the finished dish covered in dollops of brilliant green leek purée. Basmati rice is the best accompaniment for this dish.

SERVES 4

225 g/8 oz black olives (not pre-stoned)
120 g/4 oz unblanched almonds, ground
juice of a lemon
1 egg, beaten

sea salt
freshly ground black pepper
1 medium chicken (preferably free-range), quartered
2 tablespoons olive oil

For the accompanying leek purée
500 g/1 lb 2 oz thin leeks
2 tablespoons sunflower or olive oil
sea salt

To prepare the crust for the chicken, stone the olives (stone-in olives are juicier than the rubbery, pre-stoned kind) and pound them in a mortar or small pudding-basin until they begin to form a purée. Mix with the almonds, the lemon juice, the egg, a very small pinch of sea salt, and a grinding of black pepper.

Preheat the oven to 200°C/400°F, Gas mark 6. Warm an oven-proof dish in which the chicken quarters will lie side by side. Skin and de-fat the chicken quarters, heat the olive oil in a frying pan, and quickly brown the quarters on both sides. Place them in the dish and cover them with the olive and almond mixture, then bake them in the oven for 45 minutes or until the chicken is cooked through. (You can test this by piercing the flesh with a knife-point or skewer. If the juices run pink rather than transparent, the chicken is not yet completely cooked.)

After 20–25 minutes, clean the leeks, discard the base and dark green leafy parts of each one, chop them into inch lengths and place them over a moderate to low heat in a heavy, covered pan with the oil and a small pinch of sea salt. (Bring the rice, if serving, to the boil in just under twice its volume of water with a little sea salt, and leave it to simmer for 15 minutes, by which time it should have absorbed all its water and be ready to serve.) Stir the leeks and make sure that they are cooking effectively in their own steam, without sticking to the pan or drying out.

When the leeks are soft, purée them in a blender with the juices from the baked chicken. Serve the dark-crusted chicken in its dish with a dollop of bright green savoury leek purée for each person on top. Although the chicken will have given off some liquid during cooking, it will still be beautifully tender under the protective crust.

Toasted Almonds with Carrots and Courgettes

THIS IS A lovely vegetable accompaniment for fish, such as very fresh dab fillets fried in sunflower oil and well drained. The carrots and courgettes are cooked entirely in their own steam (not a difficult achievement, since courgettes have a high water content), and gain an extra delicacy and crunch from the almonds.

SERVES 3

225 g/8 oz carrots, peeled
120 g/4 oz courgettes
1 tablespoon olive oil
15 g/½ oz butter
60 g/2 oz almonds
pinch of sea salt
½ teaspoon Demerara sugar
1–2 teaspoons freshly squeezed lemon juice

Cut the carrots lengthways into strips about 2 cm/1 in long and ½ cm/¼ in wide. Cut the courgettes into similarly shaped but slightly larger strips. Heat the oil in a heavy-bottomed pan with a tight fitting lid, put in the vegetables and butter, and cover. Shake the pan well to coat all the vegetable strips with oil and butter, place very briefly over a moderate heat, shake again, then reduce this to a gentle heat. Cook for about 15 minutes, shaking the pan every now and then, but do not remove the lid if you can help it until the vegetables have given off all their steam and are cooked. They should be brilliantly coloured and tender, without the sogginess or burnt patches of courgettes fried in too much oil, or the scumminess of sliced carrots boiled fast in water.

While the vegetables are cooking, blanch the almonds and toast them in a dry pan in a medium oven (180°C/350°F, Gas mark 4) for about 10 minutes. Season the vegetables with sea salt, sugar, and lemon juice, add the almonds, shake well, and serve.

Curried Almonds

THIS MILD curry is a good light supper-dish for a summer evening, or an extra vegetarian dish, to serve, for example, alongside curried chicken. (It is also good eaten cold.) Almonds are important in the meat-based Mughal cookery of north-western India, which derives many of its traditions from courtly Persian cookery. There, almonds are generally an adjunct and a decoration to chicken pillaus and other meat dishes; yet they are also delicious, nourishing, and much lighter curried on their own.

SERVES 3–4

225 g/8 oz almonds, blanched
575 ml/1 pint water
1 large onion, peeled
1 chilli pepper, de-seeded
2 tablespoons sunflower oil
seeds from 10–12 cardamom pods
1½ teaspoons cumin seeds

1½ teaspoons coriander seeds
3 large cloves garlic, peeled and chopped
1 teaspoon sea salt
4 fresh tomatoes, skinned and roughly chopped
1½ cups/12 oz basmati rice + 2½ cups water + 1 teaspoon sea
  salt

For a simple version of almond milk, the liquid element in this dish, take 60 g/2 oz of the almonds and grind them in a liquidizer. Put the ground almonds in a pan with the water and boil steadily until the liquid is reduced by half. Strain, pressing the water from the ground almonds through a sieve, and discard the strained almonds or eat them separately.

Meanwhile, chop the onion and chilli very finely and sweat them gently in the oil for 10–15 minutes in a heavy, covered pan. Crush the cardamom, cumin, and coriander finely in a mortar and add them to the softened onion and chilli in the pan. Crush the garlic with the sea salt (since the taste of almonds is enhanced by a little salt) and stir this in. Add the tomatoes to the spice mixture in the pan. Add the whole almonds, stir well together to break up the tomatoes, cover the pan, and simmer dry while you put the rice on, bring it to the boil, and leave it to simmer.

Add the almond milk to the curry, stir well, cover, and continue simmering for the 15 minutes that it should take the rice to cook. Serve the curry on the rice, with yoghurt and cucumber *raita* and a plain lettuce or spinach salad.

Cauliflower and Almond Curry

BECAUSE OF its crunchy consistency when raw or lightly cooked, and its clean, slightly nutty taste, the much maligned cauliflower combines well with almonds. Next time you think of concocting high-cholesterol cauliflower cheese, consider this alternative. It makes a delicate-tasting light supper dish with basmati rice and chutney.

SERVES 2–3

1 tablespoon sunflower oil
1 onion, peeled and finely chopped
1 chilli pepper, de-seeded and chopped
½ cup boiling water
30 g/1 oz dried tamarind
seeds from 8–10 cardamom pods
1 teaspoon cumin seeds
1 teaspoon coriander seeds
8 g/¼ oz ginger root, peeled and chopped
2 large cloves garlic, peeled and chopped
sea salt
450 g/1 lb cauliflower, de-stalked and divided into florets
60 g/2 oz almonds, blanched
3 tablespoons Greek-style yoghurt

Heat the oil in a frying pan and lightly brown the onions. Add the chilli and cover, lowering the heat. Soften the onion and chilli together for 10 minutes while you prepare the spices. Pour boiling water over the tamarind and leave it to soak. Crush the cardamom, cumin, and coriander together in a mortar and add them to the pan; then do the same with the ginger and garlic and a little sea salt. Stir the spices into the onion and chilli, then strain on the tamarind water and push as much of the soaked tamarind pulp as you can through the strainer. Leave to cook uncovered over a gentle heat while you put on the rice. (This will cook in 15 minutes in just under twice its volume of water.) At the same time parboil the cauliflower in a little lightly salted water for 5–10 minutes until just soft, then drain it, add it to the curry sauce, and break it up into small pieces with a wooden spoon. Add the almonds and stir all well together. Cook the curry for a few minutes with the lid on, then stir in the yoghurt and serve.

For a yellower curry, add half a teaspoon of ground turmeric with the other spices. Too much turmeric, especially when it is not very fresh, can create a bitter taste.

Cauliflower and Almonds in Orange Sauce

A NOTHER EXAMPLE of the natural partnership between cauliflower and almonds, this is an adaptation of a Chilean dish, *coliflor en salsa de almendra*. Good with plain cold chicken and potatoes baked or boiled in their skins, it requires a rich, home-made chicken stock to be really successful. Ladle in the stock, if you like, straight from the stockpot after simmering it for a couple of hours, since the orange juice in the sauce should cut through any fattiness.

SERVES 3–4

1 medium/large cauliflower, washed, trimmed of base and
    leaves, and cut into 10–12 pieces
700 ml/1 ¼ pints rich chicken stock
30 g/1 oz butter
30 g/1 oz flour
juice of 1–2 oranges
120 g/4 oz almonds, blanched and lightly toasted
sea salt
freshly ground black pepper

Pack the cauliflower pieces stems downwards in a saucepan. Add
about 300 ml/½ pint well-seasoned stock, bring to the boil, cover
and boil steadily for 10 minutes, then set on one side.

Melt the butter in a heavy-bottomed pan over a low to medium
heat. Stir in the flour, then any residual cauliflower liquid. Once
this has been absorbed, stir in ladlefuls of stock until you have a
rich brown sauce. Simmer this for 5–10 minutes, then stir in the
orange juice. Break up the cauliflower pieces with a wooden spoon
and place them in a shallow heatproof dish. Cover them with a
thick scattering of almonds, then pour on the sauce. Place briefly
under a hot grill, season then serve.

Stuffed Peppers with Rice and Almond Filling

THIS DISH is barely worth making with the kind of mass-
produced tasteless red peppers from the supermarket which
collapse into watery, crumpled balloons when roasted whole. If,

however, you grow red peppers yourself or have a supply of the tastier kind, it is worth while. The almonds give protein, crunch, and a delicate flavour to the standard rice filling, and call for something gentler than the tomato sauce which is usually recommended to accompany stuffed peppers. In this dish, the peppers are topped with a brilliant light green purée of fried courgettes and whole roast garlic cloves.

SERVES 4

225 g/8 oz brown rice
1–2 teaspoons sea salt, and extra for seasoning
4 medium-sized red peppers weighing approximately 175 g/6 oz each
2 tablespoons olive oil
8–10 large cloves garlic, peeled but left whole
120 g/4 oz almonds, blanched
1 tablespoon freshly squeezed lemon juice
8–10 large leaves fresh basil (optional)
freshly ground black pepper
450 g/1 lb courgettes, sliced
1 tablespoon sunflower oil
freshly grated Parmesan

Put the rice on to boil with just under twice its volume of water and the sea salt. Reduce to simmering point and leave, tightly covered, until all the water has been absorbed. (If the rice is the untreated kind from a health-food shop, it will need 35–40 minutes simmering. Other kinds of so-called brown rice need only 25–30 minutes.)

Heat the oven to 200°C/400°F, Gas mark 6. Cut round the stem of each pepper and scoop out the seeds with the knife-blade, leaving a round opening in the base of each one. Find a roasting tin into which the peppers will fit neatly, stand them in it base-downwards, and brush them lightly with half a tablespoon of olive oil. Place the tin in the oven, and after 10 minutes reduce the heat to 180°C/350°F, Gas mark 4. Pour off any water which the peppers may have given off in roasting, replace it with a little oil, and add the garlic cloves, turning them in the oil. Return the peppers and garlic to the oven and continue roasting for another 20 minutes.

Chop the almonds roughly into halves. When the rice is cooked, stir in the almonds and add a generous tablespoon each of olive oil and lemon juice. Tear up the basil leaves, if using, and stir these into the rice mixture. Season with sea salt and freshly ground pepper to taste. Remove the peppers and garlic from the oven and reserve the garlic cloves. Arrange the softened peppers open side upwards in a high-sided ovenproof dish and spoon in the filling, pressing it well down. Cover with a piece of foil to prevent the filling from drying out, and return to the oven for 10–15 minutes.

To make the sauce, sauté the courgettes in the sunflower oil until they are soft, then purée them in a blender with the garlic cloves and a pinch of sea salt. Before serving, remove the foil from the peppers and top them with the sauce for a contrasting dish of red, whitish-fawn, and bright green. Hand round the Parmesan separately to sprinkle lavishly on top.

Almond Risotto

N OT A risotto in the conventional sense, this delicious dish makes a light, nutritious vegetarian main course for supper.

SERVES 2–3

1 large onion, peeled and chopped
4–6 sticks celery, finely chopped
2 tablespoons sunflower oil

3 tomatoes, skinned and roughly chopped
sea salt
freshly ground black pepper
Demerara sugar to taste
90 g/3 oz stone-in black olives, stoned
175 g/6 oz basmati rice
450 ml/15 fl oz water, lightly salted
15 g/½ oz butter
3 tablespoons freshly grated Parmesan
100 g/3½ oz almonds, blanched
2 eggs, hard boiled for 8–10 minutes, peeled and sliced

Soften the onion and celery in the oil for 10–15 minutes over a low to moderate heat in a heavy, covered pan. Stir in the tomatoes, raise the heat, and cook steadily for another 5–10 minutes, stirring now and again, until the tomatoes have disintegrated. Season with sea salt, freshly ground black pepper, and a little sugar if necessary, and add the olives. Simmer gently while you cook the rice in the water (about 15 minutes). Stir the butter and Parmesan into the rice, add the almonds to the sauce, and pour this over the rice. Top with the hard-boiled eggs.

Almond Pancakes

A MONG THE commonest culinary disasters are heavy pancakes made with a high proportion of flour. When cooked according to traditional English Shrove Tuesday recipes, in which all the emphasis is on a consistency which allows the pancakes to be tossed, they can be tasteless, obstinately thick about the middle, and sometimes blackened as a result of vain attempts to cook them through. 'Wholefood' pancakes, made with wholemeal flour, can be leaden, with a tendency to fall apart; white flour pancakes stickily bland.

Being fond of pancakes, I discovered in the end that there are other ingredients which make it possible to bypass flour altogether. Oat flakes, ground to a coarse flour in a liquidizer, make light, pale, nutty-tasting pancakes with none of the heaviness associated with wheat flour. Wheatgerm, ground up finely, either on its own or combined with ground oats, makes golden, sweet-tasting pancakes. (French wheatgerm is best, since it comes so finely ground in the packet that you can mix it directly into pancake batter: a great advantage when cooking without electrical equipment.) Almonds, ground up with half their weight in oat flakes, make nutritious, crunchy-textured pancakes, slightly heavier than those made with oats alone, but the best and most interesting in terms of taste. They are good on their own; as a light, savoury lunch dish (for example, wrapped round spoonfuls of grated carrot salad dressed with sesame oil and balsamic vinegar); or as a dessert, enclosing helpings of not too sugary home-made whole berry jam or preserved fruit such as blackberry or strawberry, accompanied by large spoonfuls of Greek-style yoghurt to mingle with the juices.

MAKES 16–20 PANCAKES

120 g/4 oz unblanched almonds
60 g/2 oz oat flakes
4 eggs
6 tablespoons sunflower oil
260–280 ml/just under 10 fl oz milk

After grinding the almonds and oats together, whisk the eggs in a bowl, add the oil and milk, and then stir in the almond mixture. This is a better method than whizzing everything up together in a blender, since it avoids the formation of a solid, heavy residue at the bottom of the liquidizer goblet. Be sparing with the milk at first; it is easy enough to dilute a thickish batter, but much more difficult to thicken a too thin one.

Heat a lightly oiled pancake- or chappati-pan to just below the maximum heat for your ring. When the oil in the centre of the pan begins to dry out, brush a piece of oily greaseproof paper across it and pour in 2–3 tablespoons of the pancake batter. If this is thin enough, small holes should appear in the pancake when you tilt the pan to spread out the batter in a circular shape. Lower the heat slightly and leave the pancake for a minute or two until it begins to bubble up, then loosen it all round the edges and then underneath with a palette-knife, turn it and cook it for 20–25 seconds on the other side. Have a plate warming in a low oven and keep the pancakes stacked on it in the oven until all are cooked. Re-oil the pan for succeeding pancakes, keeping the batter well stirred and thinning it with a little extra milk towards the end.

Almond Cake (1)

THIS IS the purest form of almond cake, with no butter or flour in the mixture. The cake, a rather flat one, deeply golden inside and dark brown on top, has a heavenly spongey texture and a rich but not too sweet taste. Although basing my recipe on a Majorcan one (from Elizabeth Carter's *Majorcan Food and Cookery*), I have halved the amount of sugar given, since I find that the traditional southern European practice of making almond cakes with equal quantities of almonds and sugar, or even more sugar than almonds, results in an unbearable level of sweetness.

SERVES 4–5

175 g/6 oz unblanched almonds, ground (see method)
90 g/3 oz Demerara sugar
3 eggs, separated
2 tablespoons Greek-style yoghurt
½ teaspoon cinnamon

Grease a 20-cm/8-in sponge tin, ideally with a spring clip. Pre-heat the oven to 180°C/350°F, Gas mark 4. If you, can, grind the almonds yourself in a blender rather than using shop-bought ground ones. Home-ground almonds can be interestingly uneven in texture as well as fresher than ready-ground ones; and there is no need in this recipe to blanch them. Tip the almonds into a bowl, add the sugar, beaten egg yolks, yoghurt, and cinnamon, and mix well. Whisk the egg whites until stiff, then fold them into the mixture. Bake for 30–40 minutes, testing for doneness with a fork after 25–30 minutes, and cover the top with foil if it is becoming a very deep brown. Cool in the tin for half an hour, then turn out upside-down on to a rack.

A moist, nourishing cake with a delicately spicy flavour, this is particularly good served with coffee, Greek-style yoghurt, fruit, or ice-cream.

Almond Cake (2)

A SLIGHTLY solider cake than the previous one, but still very rich and good. The combination of almond and lemon is a springlike one; but if instead you prefer a lightly gingery flavour, reminiscent of English seventeenth-century almond gingerbread, leave out the lemon zest and juice and add instead a glass of ginger wine or a tablespoon of ginger juice with honey, obtainable from Culpeper herbalists' shops. In this case, reduce the amount of sugar to 45 g/1½ oz. The proportion of almonds to flour in this cake is roughly inverse to that given in old-fashioned English recipes, in which the flour was the main ingredient and the scarce, expensive almonds added only for a slight variation in texture and delicacy in flavour, often boosted with a few bitter almonds or with commercial almond essence.

SERVES 6

60 g/2 oz butter
60 g/2 oz wholemeal flour
175 g/6 oz unblanched almonds, ground, + 8–10 halved
   almonds
60 g/2 oz Demerara sugar
2 eggs, separated
zest and juice of ½ a lemon

Pre-heat the oven to 180°C/350°F/Gas mark 4. Rub the butter into the flour, add all the almonds, the sugar, and the beaten egg yolks, and stir in the lemon zest and juice. Whisk the egg whites until stiff and fold them in. Line a small rectangular loaf tin with oiled greaseproof paper, spoon in the cake mixture, and bake for half an hour or longer, testing for doneness with a fork after 25–30 minutes.

Almond Lemon Cheesecake

THIS LEMONY almond pie in fact contains no cheese, but has a texture roughly similar to that of the lightest kind of cheesecake. I find it fresh-tasting and delicious, with a good contrast between the light lemon-flavoured filling and the chewy, nutty base.

SERVES 4

For the base
30 g/1 oz butter
60 g/2 oz Demerara sugar
2 tablespoons milk
60 g/2 oz oat flakes
60 g/2 oz unblanched almonds, ground

For the filling
3 eggs, separated
60 g/2 oz Demerara sugar
zest and juice of 1 lemon
120 g/4 oz unblanched almonds, ground

To make the base, melt the butter in a small heavy-bottomed saucepan, stir in the sugar, then add the milk. Bring this briefly to the boil, stirring as you do so, and simmer for a few minutes until you have a thick, butterscotch-tasting mixture. Stir in the oats and almonds, remove from the heat, then turn out into an oiled 20-cm/ 8-in sponge tin, ideally with a spring clip. Leave the mixture to cool slightly for a minute or two, then flatten it over the base of the tin, pushing it down with wetted palms or with your knuckles. While quite sticky, this mixture is also pliable; and, like the filling, it has the advantage of needing little baking, being already partly cooked.

To make the filling, mix the egg yolks, sugar, and lemon zest in a bowl which will fit over a saucepan of boiling water and beat them together until light. Set the oven to 200°C/400°F/Gas mark 6. Over the boiling water, add the lemon juice and whisk until the mixture has puffed up and is frothy. Remove from the heat and beat in the almonds. Whisk the whites until stiff and fold these in. Turn out the filling at once to cover the prepared base and smooth down the surface with a knife until the filling touches the oiled sides of the sponge tin. (This is not a conventional tart; and the base, like pizza dough or the cracker-crumb base of a cheesecake, should line only the bottom of the tin without coming up the sides.) Bake for 10 minutes in the preheated oven, then lower the heat to 170°C/325°F/Gas mark 3, and leave for a further 10–15 minutes. Remove from the oven, loosen around the edge with a knife, and leave to cool in the tin before turning out.

Yeasted Almond Cake

Yeasted cakes, like the Polish and Russian Easter cakes, the French *brioche*, the Italian *panettone*, and (in a cruder class) the English lardy-cake, have always had a special fascination for me. Their springy, pliable texture, so unlike the compacted or drily crumbly texture of moist English fruit cake or eggy sponge, looks back to a long-lost period in English baking: the period of Simnel cakes, wigs, and Sally Lunns, light, sweetened, yeasted cakes which all but disappeared half-way through the nineteenth century, surviving chiefly in the rapidly staling form of the baker's Chelsea or Bath Bun.

This yeasted cake is made chiefly of almonds, which adds to its interest and nutritional value and gives it a dense yet light texture. It contains no butter or margarine, and needs only a little almond oil for a delicate taste and additional keeping quality. Sunflower oil, or any other bland oil, will do as a second-best option.

SERVES 6–8

120 g/4 oz strong white flour
225 g/8 oz unblanched almonds, ground
1 pinch sea salt
1 rounded teaspoon/2–3 g easy-bake yeast
60 g/2 oz Demerara or soft brown sugar
½ teaspoon cinnamon
3 tablespoons almond or sunflower oil
60 g/2 oz raisins
60 g/2 oz good-quality candied peel, finely chopped
2 egg yolks (less ½ egg yolk for glazing)
4–6 tablespoons lukewarm milk

For the glaze
½ egg yolk
1–2 teaspoons milk

Combine the flour and almonds in a mixing-bowl with the sea salt, yeast, sugar, and cinnamon. Rub in the oil, then stir in the raisins, candied peel, egg yolks, and milk. The mixture will be on the sticky side. Work it in the bowl for 10 minutes with the fingers of one hand, scraping it away from the sides to form it into a cohesive ball, and adding an extra sprinkling of flour if this seems necessary to get the mixture moving. Cover the bowl with a clean tea towel or cling film and leave in a warm place for an hour, then place the mixture in a round, oiled 20-cm/8-in sponge-tin, flatten it into a circular cake, and glaze it with the egg and milk mixture. Set the oven to 210°C/425°F/Gas mark 7, place the cake in it directly, and bake it for 35–40 minutes, reducing the heat slightly after the first 15 minutes. Serve warm, with butter, or cold.

Almond and Poppyseed Cake (1)

A YEASTED loaf of enriched and sweetened dough, baked round a filling of ground, sweetened poppy seeds which have been softened in warm flavoured milk, is a traditional German and central European treat. I have made this version of it special by mixing the poppy seeds with egg white and ground almonds, which reduces the concentrated harshness of their taste, and blending ground almonds into the dough to make this extra rich. If you can use almond oil as the shortening, it gives a delicacy to the taste of the dough comparable with that of real vanilla as a flavour for the filling.

SERVES 4

For the dough

200 g/7 oz strong white flour

120 g/4 oz unblanched almonds, ground

1 teaspoon easy-bake yeast

1 teaspoon sea salt

30 g/1 oz Demerara sugar

2 egg yolks

1 tablespoon almond oil *or* melted butter (omit salt if butter is salted)

150 ml/5 fl oz lukewarm milk

For the filling
30 g/1 oz poppy seeds, ground
150 ml/5 fl oz milk
45 g/1½ oz Demerara sugar
½ a vanilla pod, split (optional)
75 g/2½ oz unblanched almonds, ground
2 egg whites, beaten (less 1 tablespoon, see below)

To finish
1 tablespoon beaten egg white
6–8 almonds, blanched and split

To make the dough, pour 175 g/6 oz of the flour into a mixing-bowl and add the almonds. Stir in the yeast, a pinch of sea salt (unless you are using salted butter), and the Demerara sugar. Mix in the egg yolks, the almond oil or melted butter, and the milk. Stir the mixture or work it with your hands (it will be stiff but quite sticky), then gradually work in the last 30 g/1 oz of flour, using the fingers of one hand, until the dough forms a ball which comes away cleanly from the side of the bowl. Cover and leave in a warm place for about an hour.

To make the filling, grind the poppy seeds in a blender and put them in a small heavy saucepan with the milk, the sugar, and vanilla (if using). Bring to the boil, stir well, and turn down the heat to simmering point. Leave for 5–10 minutes until the mixture has thickened. When the vanilla pod has softened slightly, scrape away as much as you can of the soft lining and mix this with the poppy seeds, sugar, and milk before discarding the pod. Stir in the almonds and egg white, keeping back a tablespoon of egg white when you do so.

Stretch and pat the rested dough between your hands, shaping it into a square about 1 cm/½ in thick and 30 cm/12 in on each side, then place it on a floured board and flatten it gently with your hands until it is about half as large again. Oil a loaf-tin. Spoon the filling on to the centre of the dough and spread it towards the edges. Fold in the top and bottom edges of the square towards the centre, then join the side edges together as if making a parcel. Lift the filled dough into the loaf tin and cram it down as best you can. (There is no need for any great delicacy at this point; if the filling bursts through the dough, this can always be patched with a spare piece from one end.) Brush the top with the reserved egg white, decorate it if you like with blanched split almonds, then place the tin in the oven and set the heat to 210°C/425°F/Gas mark 7. Allow the loaf to rise as the oven warms, and leave it in for about 30 minutes once the oven is hot. Cover the top with foil after 15–20 minutes, and turn down the heat 10 minutes before the end.

Almond and Poppyseed Cake (2)

A NOTHER VERSION of this cake, square and juicily well filled, which you can make with left-over dough from baking your own bread. The inspiration is Hungarian. The cake, really a kind of turnover, fills a 20-cm/8-in square tin and keeps well for several days without needing to be sealed in an airtight container. A hearty health-food version works very well with my favourite bread mix of part wholemeal, part brown malted grain flour. (A good, interesting version of the latter is Cotswold Crunch, from F. W. P. Matthews Ltd, millers, of Shipton-under-Wychwood, Oxfordshire.) Other, more traditional, recipes for this cake can be found in George Lang's *The Cuisine of Hungary*.

SERVES 6

340 g/12 oz yeasted bread dough (or see below)
120 g/4 oz poppy seeds, ground

250 ml/8 fl oz milk
120 g/4 oz Demerara sugar
zest of 1 lemon
120 g/4 oz almonds, blanched or unblanched, ground
whites of 2 eggs, stiffly beaten
60 g/2 oz raisins

For the glaze
2 teaspoons egg yolk
1 tablespoon milk

When the bread dough has risen, roll it out as flat as you can on a well-floured board until it forms a large square. To make the filling, add the poppy seeds to the milk in a saucepan, bring to the boil, stir well, and simmer for 10–15 minutes. Add the sugar, lemon zest, and almonds (which need not be blanched before grinding if you do not mind a certain mild grittiness). Fold in the egg whites. Sprinkle the raisins over the square of dough and press them in gently. Now spoon about two-thirds of the filling on to the dough, spread it out, and lift up the edge of the dough nearest to you, bringing it over to join the opposite edge to form a soft oblong parcel. Place the rest of the filling on top of the centre of the oblong and bring up the two side pieces to enclose it. You will now have a two-layered turnover encased in a thin outer skin of dough. Being very soft, this will be difficult to lift; so invert the oiled tin over it, support this with an outspread hand, and turn the board upside-down so that the turnover settles into the tin with its neat underside uppermost. Brush this with two teaspoons of egg yolk mixed into a tablespoon of milk to glaze, and bake in an oven preheated to 210°C/425°F, Gas mark 7, for 30–35 minutes. Serve cold, preferably the day after baking when the flavours will have mellowed a little, either plain as a coffee cake or as a dessert with Greek-style yoghurt.

If you do not make your own bread but still want to try this cake, place 225 g/8 oz strong white flour, or a mixture of strong white and strong wholemeal or malted grain flour, in a bowl with a pinch of sea salt and ⅔ of a teaspoon of easy-bake dried yeast. Make a well in the centre, pour in 2 tablespoons of sunflower oil and rub this in, then repeat the well and pour in 120 ml/5 fl oz tepid water. Mix together until the dough forms a consistent ball, adding more flour if necessary. Turn out on to a lightly floured board and knead for 10 minutes, then replace in the bowl, cover with a clean tea towel, and leave in a warm place to rise for an hour.

Almond Biscuits

RECIPES FOR almond biscuits vary, from exquisitely curled, rich, sweet *tuiles aux amandes*, made with butter, flour, sugar, and egg white, to macaroons, consisting purely of ground almonds, sugar, and egg white, and to more rugged alternatives such as these solid, but deliciously soft and chewy, almond biscuits made with yoghurt. Using cream instead of yoghurt makes the biscuits very crisp, if less digestible and healthy.

MAKES 10–12 BISCUITS

200 g/7 oz almonds, blanched or unblanched (see below), ground
90 g/3 oz oat flakes
100 g/3½ oz Demerara or golden granulated sugar
120 g/4 oz Greek-style yoghurt, *or* yoghurt and cream

Put the almonds in a bowl. Blanched almonds will make the biscuits very soft and golden; unblanched ones, more interestingly textured but speckled with dark brown. Mix in the oats and sugar, then the yoghurt, until the mixture forms a ball. Preheat the oven to 180°C/350°F, Gas mark 4. Have ready a well-oiled baking sheet. Sprinkle some oat flakes on a board, flatten the ball of dough on top of them with the heel of one hand, sprinkle it with more oat flakes, turn it over, and roll it out as thinly as you can. Cut out circles and place these, just touching one another, on the baking sheet. Bake for about 20 minutes until the biscuits are golden-brown, then turn one over with a spatula. If it is dark brown underneath, remove the biscuits immediately to cool outside the oven on the baking sheet. If it still looks pale, turn off the heat and leave the biscuits in the cooling oven for another 5–10 minutes before removing to cool on the baking sheet. If you prefer your biscuits soft, transfer them straight from the oven to a rack or plate. These biscuits are not too sugary, and have a true almond taste with the slight elasticity at the centre of good macaroons.

Almond Tiles or Crisps

THE CLASSIC French recipe for very thin, rich, curled almond biscuits to accompany desserts.

MAKES 12–16 BISCUITS

60 g/2 oz butter
120 g/4 oz soft brown sugar
2 egg whites, stiffly beaten
120 g/4 oz white pastry flour
90 g/3 oz almonds, blanched and ground
½ teaspoon almond or vanilla extract (optional)
60 g/2 oz almonds, blanched and slivered

Preheat the oven to 210°C/425°F, Gas mark 7. Have ready 3–4 well-greased baking sheets, as the batter for these biscuits is liquid and needs space to spread.

Cream the butter and sugar, then fold in the egg whites. Sieve in the flour, then fold this into the mixture with the ground almonds and any additional flavouring. Drop half-teaspoonfuls of the mixture on to the baking sheets, spacing them well apart, then spread them out with the back of a wet spoon until very thin. Top each one with a sprinkling of slivered almonds and bake for 4–5 minutes until the edges are just browned.

While the biscuits are still warm, free each one from the baking sheet and mould it into a curved, semi-circular tile shape over a bottle or rolling pin. Make sure that the biscuits do not cool before you remove them from the tin, or they will set rigid before they can be moulded. Leave the biscuits to cool on racks.

Almond and Ginger Macaroon Biscuits

A LMONDS AND ginger were often combined in seventeenth-century English cooking, giving rise to recipes for 'white ginger bread of almonds' and other such delicacies. Once you have become used to the idea, a touch of real ginger seems infinitely preferable to artificial-tasting almond or vanilla essence for adding depth and interest to the flavour of almonds. Unblanched almonds give these macaroons a slight ruggedness which suits their ginger flavour.

MAKES 10–12 BISCUITS

200 g/7 oz unblanched almonds, ground
90 g/3 oz Demerara or soft brown sugar
1 tablespoon ready-made ginger syrup, e.g. Culpeper Ginger
    Juice with Honey (from Culpeper shops in the UK)
2 egg whites, stiffly beaten

Preheat the oven to 180°C/350°F, Gas mark 4. Have ready two large very well-oiled baking sheets. In a bowl, mix together the almonds, sugar, and ginger syrup and fold in the egg whites. With wet hands, form the mixture into balls the size of half an egg, press these flat on the palm of one hand, transfer them to one of the tins, and flatten them again with wet fingers when in place to form biscuits about 6.5 cm/2½ in in diameter. Bake for 20–25 minutes until the biscuits are golden-brown and glossy, then remove from the oven and cool in the tins. When the biscuits have hardened, remove them carefully with a metal palette knife. Store in an airtight container.

Chocolate, Almond, and Walnut Biscuits

THESE ARE not really biscuits but small, fudgy, nutty, soft cakes. They can be compulsive eating at any time of day, but are nourishing as well as energizing, and have an adult taste of bitter chocolate and nuts rather than the cloying sweetness of many commercially produced chocolate concoctions. You can make a simpler version using 1½ tablespoons of cocoa powder instead of the chocolate and water; but the higher the quality of chocolate used, the better, naturally, the biscuits will taste. This mixture of nuts strikes a balance between the fine sweet chewiness and dryness of almonds and the oilier robuster bitterness of walnuts.

MAKES 8–10 BISCUITS

60 g/2 oz plain dark chocolate (preferably 70% cocoa solids), broken up
30 g/1 oz butter
1 tablespoon cold water
75 g/2½ oz Demerara sugar
120 g/4 oz unblanched almonds, ground
90 g/3 oz walnut halves, ground
2 egg whites, stiffly beaten

Melt the chocolate and butter in the water in a heavy-bottomed pan over a low to moderate heat. Stir in the sugar and nuts. Remove from the heat and fold in the egg whites. Set the oven to 180°C/350°F, Gas mark 4. Drop spoonfuls of the mixture on to well-oiled baking sheets, spreading them out with wet fingertips into biscuit-shaped rounds. Bake for 5 minutes, then turn off the heat and remove the biscuits from the oven. They should by now be glossy and beginning to harden. Turn them over with a spatula and return them to the cooling oven for a few minutes, then cool on their tins in the open air.

Almond Sorbet

A LOVELY thick sorbet with a slightly chewy texture, more like the Indian *kulfi* than a conventional Western-style water ice. Home-ground almonds give a more interesting texture to this sorbet than the packeted ground variety bought in shops.

225 g/8 oz almonds, blanched and coarsely ground
90 g/3 oz thick white honey
60 g/2 oz brown sugar
4 tablespoons water
2–3 tablespoons rose-water or fresh lemon or lime juice

Put the almonds in a bowl and mix them thoroughly with the honey. A thick whitish honey, such as clover or rape-seed, gives a lighter colour and gentler flavour than most golden-brown honeys. Boil the sugar in the water for 4–5 minutes until it has formed a thin syrup and reduced to 3 tablespoons in all. Mix this with the almonds and honey, then stir in the rose-water or juice. Flatten down the stiffish almond paste in a lidded plastic container or Pyrex dish, and enclose in a plastic bag if the lid does not seal. Place in the freezer and leave for several hours or overnight. This sorbet needs no stirring, and sets to a slightly soft, malleable consistency. Serve with plain yeasted almond cake, or with a chocolate- or pistachio-flavoured cream. The rose-water version is particularly good eaten as a sweet, with lots of Greek-style yoghurt.

Paskha

THE SUBSTANCE of this recipe comes from Nina Petrova's *Russian Cookery* (1968). *Paskha*, meaning 'Easter', is the traditional celebratory food of the Russian Easter. A fine, light, vanilla-flavoured cheese cream, enriched with egg yolks, butter, sugar, and chopped almonds, it is often eaten with *kulich*, a yeasted sultana and almond cake. The Russian moulds for draining *paskha* were made of five pieces of wood slotted together in an inverted pyramidal shape, decorated with the letters XX and BB for *Khristos Voskrese*, the Russian ritual Easter greeting, 'Christ is risen'.

SERVES 6–7

3 egg yolks
310 g/11 oz Demerara sugar
150 ml/5 fl oz milk
½ vanilla pod, slit along one side
120 g/4 oz butter, in small pieces
800 g/1¾ lb curd cheese
grated lemon zest (optional)
60 g/2 oz almonds, blanched and finely chopped
4 tablespoons double cream, whipped

Beat the egg yolks with 120 g/4 oz of the sugar until white. Add the milk and the half vanilla pod and continue beating together in a bowl over a saucepan of boiling water until you have a thick vanilla-flavoured custard. Once the vanilla pod has softened, scrape out the tiny seeds and add these to the mixture to increase the flavour. Discard the pod. Beat in the butter, then remove from the heat and cool.

Sieve the cheese into a large bowl. Add the rest of the sugar (much of which will eventually drain away), lemon zest if using, almonds, and cream. Line a colander or other pierced receptacle with clean wet muslin, stand this in a basin to catch the liquid, pour in the *paskha*, and fold the muslin over the top. Press down using a plate with a small weight on the top placed over the muslin. Leave overnight or for several hours in a cool place to drain, then turn out the *paskha* on to a dish, cover it with a damp napkin, and keep it in the fridge. It should keep for about a week if the napkin is renewed every day.

Coffee Almond Pudding

HALF SOUFFLÉ, half thick custard, this pudding is best eaten cold.

SERVES 4

5 eggs, separated
120 g/4 oz Demerara sugar
5–6 tablespoons strong black coffee
150 g/5 oz almonds, blanched
90 g/3 oz Mascarpone or curd cheese

Place the egg yolks, sugar, and coffee in a bowl over a saucepan of simmering water and beat for about 10 minutes until the mixture is thick. Grind 115 g/4 oz of the almonds and mix them with the Mascarpone or curd cheese. Lightly toast and split the remaining almonds.

Set the oven to 190°C/375°F, Gas mark 5. Stir the curd cheese and ground almonds into the coffee and egg yolk mixture, then fold in the stiffly beaten egg whites. Pour into an oiled ovenproof dish and bake for 12–15 minutes. When the surface has begun to set, scatter on the toasted almonds and return to the oven for a few minutes longer. Cool and serve cold, but not chilled.

Nougat

NOBODY SEEMS to know quite when some inspired person thought of including stiffly beaten egg whites in the nougat made at Montélimar in Provence. A simple cake of chopped nuts bound together with a syrup of sugar or honey, related to the Greek *baklava*, seems to have existed in that area for centuries, and is the kind described as nougat in many cookery books, even as recently as Elisabeth Luard's *European Festival Food* (1990). The original nuts were probably walnuts; and it was only in the seventeenth century, some decades after Olivier de Serres, a Provençal landowner, had introduced almond cultivation on to his estate at Pradel, near Montélimar, that the local product began to be made with almonds. 'White nougat' (possibly a reference to the colour of blanched almonds rather than of egg white) then became an inescapable present for any dignitary passing through this town on the main road south through the Rhône Valley: 1 cwt for the French royal princes visiting in 1701, 56 lb for their ducal companions, and 22 lb for the Persian ambassador a few years later.

To Eliza Acton, writing in the 1840s, nougat was a kind of confectioner's almond brittle held together with a minimal quantity of sugar syrup. (Her recipe calls for 6 oz sugar to 12 oz blanched, toasted, split almonds.) 'Nougat baskets' were fashionable in Victorian times for holding sweets on grand dinner-tables, and may have gone uneaten until later, in the kitchen. Charles Elmé Francatelli, in the *Royal Confectioner* (1874), repeats Eliza Acton's simple recipe, but adds another, called *Nougat de Marseilles*, containing 1¼ lb of almonds to 8 oz each of sugar and honey, 3 egg whites and ½ gill of orange flower water, specifying that this should dry out on wafer (i.e. rice) paper. It is the thickening of beaten egg white, holding its light, airy shape when the hot syrup is added to it, and then studded with almond or other nut pieces and compressed, that gives Montélimar nougat its particular mystery and charm, and must account for its popularity among the sweet-eating British and other Europeans as well as the French.

If you do not have rice paper in the house when making nougat, this does not matter unless you hope to store the nougat in boxes or give it away as presents. Nougat of the right consistency will set semi-hard on a plate, preferably oiled with almond oil, and can easily be cut up and removed for home consumption. Almonds are the classic ingredient of nougat (the Montélimar kind must consist of at least 30% almonds, or 28% almonds with 2% pistachios, and 25% honey); but Brazil nuts and untoasted hazelnuts also go well in it. Toasted hazelnuts produce a very sweet taste. The only special item of equipment which you will need for nougat-making is a balloon whisk, essential for keeping the egg whites well whisked with one hand while you pour in the hot syrup with the other.

SERVES 8–10

60 g/2 oz honey
175 g/6 oz light-coloured sugar (e.g. unrefined golden
    granulated)
2 egg whites
100 g/3½ oz almonds, blanched, or hazelnuts, skinned
rice paper *or* almond oil

Spread out the almonds or hazelnuts on a baking tray and toast them in a moderate oven, 180°C/350°F, Gas mark 4, for 15 minutes or until lightly browned, then chop them roughly on a board. Meanwhile put the honey and sugar in a heavy-bottomed saucepan and heat them gradually until they form a bubbling syrup. Whisk the egg whites until stiff in a large pudding basin, and prepare a saucepan of simmering water over which the basin will fit. When the syrup sets hard on contact with cold water, remove it from the heat and pour it gradually into the egg whites, whisking all the time. Place the bowl of egg whites and syrup over the pan of simmering water and continue whisking for 5–10 minutes until you have a dense, white, sticky mass which coheres to the inside of the bowl. Remove from the heat and continue whisking for a further few minutes, gradually adding the chopped nuts, until the balloon whisk becomes completely clogged and you have to discard it in favour of a knife. Beat for a little longer with the knife, scraping off any nougat which has begun to set on the inside of the bowl. (Francatelli specifies that at this stage nougat should be beaten for three hours.) Its texture should by now be elastic and chewy. *Either* line a tin with rice paper, pour in the nougat, cover with more rice paper, and weigh down overnight, *or* set between two plates oiled with almond oil.

Quince Nougat

I T IS POSSIBLE to make nougat in a soft, un-chewy form, especially when the proportion of sugar to egg whites is on the small side. If your nougat has turned out soft, it can be put to good use in a creamy nougat-flavoured pudding. Here is a good one for when quinces are available in October or November.

SERVES 5–6

3 medium/large quinces (in all, approx 900 g/2 lb) peeled
450 ml/15 fl oz water

5–6 heaped tablespoons soft nougat (see page 54)
30 g/1 oz toasted, flaked almonds (optional)

Cut the quinces vertically into quarters, then cut through each quarter horizontally, coring as you go. Put the cut-up quinces in a saucepan, cover with the water, bring to the boil, and simmer for 20 minutes, or until nearly all the water has been absorbed. Blend the quince flesh into the remaining water, turn out the purée into a bowl, and leave it to cool before adding the nougat.

This pudding tastes delectable, but can look uninteresting if you stir all the nougat directly into the quince purée. Keep back a tablespoon or two of the nougat to decorate the surface, and sprinkle this, if you like, with flaked toasted almonds.

Quince and Almond Cream

THIS IS A solid but truly delicate-tasting autumn pudding. Quinces and almonds, both products of Spain, seem made to complement one another. The flavour of the quince, lightly sweetened and conveyed chiefly through its smell, brings out an equal fineness in the taste of the almonds.

SERVES 5–6

2 medium quinces (in all, approx 570 g/1¼ lb), peeled
300 ml/10 fl oz water
100 g/3½ oz almonds, blanched
250 ml/8 fl oz milk

2 egg yolks
100 g/3½ oz Demerara sugar

Cut the quinces vertically into quarters, then cut through each quarter horizontally, coring as you go. Cover the quinces with the water in a saucepan, bring to the boil, cover, and simmer for 20 minutes. Mash the softened flesh into the remaining liquid; or, if you like a very smooth purée, liquidize it.

Keep 12–15 of the almonds whole and grind up the rest in a blender. Split the whole almonds and (if you like) toast them in a medium oven until they are pale brown.

Bring the milk to just under boiling point, reduce the heat to low, and whisk in the egg yolks. Stir gently and continuously with a wooden spoon until you have a thickish custard. Strain this over the quince purée, then add the sugar and ground almonds and mix well. Turn the pudding into a soufflé dish or similar ovenproof container and decorate the top with the split whole almonds. Bake in a bain-marie in a low to medium oven, 170°C/325°F, Gas mark 3, for 20–30 minutes until the surface of the pudding has turned a light golden colour. Serve warm or at room temperature, not chilled.

Sweet, Spicy Spinach Tart

A CLASSIC seventeenth-century English dish, from a period when sweet, semi-sweet, and savoury dishes were laid out on the dinner table side by side, and when every good homely dinner included some kind of fruit or custard tart. At that time spinach, on account of its smooth texture and exotic origins, was still regarded as enough of a delicacy to be lightened, sweetened, spiced, and enclosed in a crust. (For a parallel instance, see recipes for the traditional Catalan dish of spinach with pine nuts and raisins, *espinacs amb panses y piñons*, as given by Patience Gray in *Honey From a Weed* (1986), and by others.) A simpler mixture, consisting of cooked spinach, sugar, beaten egg, and spices, could be fried in spoonfuls in butter as sweet spinach fritters. Such dishes were favourite items in the kind of ladies' cookery which well-to-do women indulged in for enjoyment and described in the handwritten cookery books which they passed down the family to be added to from generation to generation.

This recipe is adapted from one in a MS cookery book in the British Library. Traditionally the spinach was boiled and drained, mixed with ground almonds, rose-water, currants, beaten eggs, and sugar, and seasoned with powdered cinnamon and ginger, before being baked in a pastry case. For a spicier flavour I have substituted a ginger syrup for the sugar, cinnamon, and powdered ginger, and crushed cardamom for the currants. A more faithful version of the traditional recipe can be found in Hilary Spurling's *Elinor Fettiplace's Receipt Book* (1986).

SERVES 5–6

60 g/2 oz fresh ginger, peeled and chopped
100 g/3½ oz Demerara sugar
250 ml/8 fl oz water
90 g/3 oz butter
175 g/6 oz strong white flour
675 g/1½ lb fresh spinach (not chard) *or* 450 g/1 lb frozen
   spinach
sea salt
90 g/3 oz Greek-style yoghurt
100 g/3½ oz almonds, blanched or unblanched, ground
seeds from 5–6 cardamom pods, crushed
3 eggs, beaten

Put the ginger in a small heavy saucepan with the sugar and bruise it with the tip of a wooden spoon until the ginger juice has begun to soak into the sugar. Cover with the water, bring to the boil, and simmer for 20–25 minutes. Strain through a hand-operated *moulin-légumes* or food mill, incorporating as much as you can of the fibreless ginger residue which comes through. This syrup is extra strong, since it loses some flavour in baking.

Meanwhile rub the butter into the flour and add just enough very cold water to make a ball of firm, pliable pastry. Set the oven to 210°C/425°F, Gas mark 7. Roll out the pastry on a floured board to line a greased 25-cm/10-in flan dish or tin, and bake blind for 10 minutes.

Wash the spinach thoroughly if fresh, boil it rapidly for 5–10 minutes in a large covered saucepan with a small pinch of sea salt and the water left on the leaves from the last rinse, and drain it thoroughly, pressing out the liquid with a wooden spatula or spoon. Chop finely and mix in the strained ginger syrup, yoghurt, almonds, cardamom seeds, and eggs. Put this mixture into the pastry case, turn the oven down to 190°C/375°F, Gas mark 5, and bake the tart for another 25–30 minutes until the filling is firm and has slightly risen. Leave to cool before serving, but avoid refrigerating. Keep in a cool place and eat within a day or two of baking. The crust should be crisp and the filling a pleasantly nutty, dense, spicy-tasting mass of speckled light and dark green.

I have made this tart with frozen spinach instead of fresh, and have found it less succulent but still acceptable. If doing this, put the spinach to cook as directed on the packet while you make the pastry and bake it blind. When the spinach is cooked, add a little water, then mix in the other ingredients and proceed as before.

Apple Hedgehog

A TRADITIONAL English pudding of moulded cooked apple covered with egg white, custard, or whipped cream and stuck all over with slivered blanched almonds to resemble prickles.

There are various complicated instructions about how to make this pudding. Most agree on one point, that the basis of the hedgehog is composed of sweetened, cooked apple, which should be consistent enough to stay mounded up in a hedgehog-shape when cold. I have devised my own ingredients for making a hedgehog, introducing an extra almond layer which both improves the texture and taste of the dish and makes it easier for the little animal to hold its shape when warm and when cooling down.

SERVES 5–6

900 g/2 lb well-ripened Bramley Apples

45 g/1½ oz butter

90–100 g/3–3½ oz + 45 g/1½ oz Demerara sugar

2 egg whites, beaten until firm

120 g/4 oz almonds, unblanched, ground + 60 g/2 oz
    almonds, blanched and halved lengthways

142 ml/5 fl oz carton double or whipping cream, whipped

Peel, core, and slice the apples. Melt the butter in a large heavy pan with a lid and add the apples and 90 g/3 oz sugar. If your apples are large, well-ripened Bramleys they should not need more than 90 g/3 oz; but sour apples will need a tablespoon or two extra. Cook the apples, covered, over a gentle to moderate heat, stirring once or twice, for 8–10 minutes. By the end of this time the slices should have just begun to disintegrate, but most of them should still keep a recognizable shape.

Butter an oblong pie-dish and mound up the apples in it, keeping them away from the sides and using the solider slices to give the structure a high domelike oblong shape. Preheat the oven to 190°C/375°F, Gas mark 5. Mix together the egg whites, the almonds, and the remaining sugar and smooth this mixture over the top and sides of the mounded cooked apple with a wet knife. Bake for 15–20 minutes, or until the almond meringue layer has hardened into a shell. Remove from the oven, cool, then gently decant on to a plate, if necessary by turning the pudding upside-down and then inverting it over a second plate so that the almond meringue layer is once more on top. In baking, the apple will have spread sideways beyond the bounds imposed on it by the meringue layer; so improve the hedgehog shape by spooning apple from the sides on top of the meringue, converting this into a central layer.

When the pudding is completely cool, mask with whipped cream and cover with rows of blanched almond slivers stuck in vertically to resemble prickles. Serve at room temperature rather than refrigerating, since this brings out the warmth and natural sweetness of the apples.

Almond Drink

I HAD LONG been intrigued by Ethel Ow's cooking at Munchy Munchy, a small, reassuringly quiet and plain restaurant in Park End Street, near Oxford Station, before I began to ask her about her methods. There are always half a dozen main dishes on the menu, which changes daily; and they are listed by their ingredients rather than by exotic names. On my birthday one year, for lunch there, I ate a chicken dish made with garam masala (Indian mixed spices), sour cream, slivered almonds, dried apricots, and fresh coriander. Beef, lamb, chicken, duck, fish, and seafood dishes contain individualistic combinations of flavourings and, often, a thickening of appropriate ground or slivered nuts. As

I expected, Ethel devotes a great deal of thought to developing her recipes, combining the cooking of her native Indonesia with family traditions handed down by her Dutch great-grandmother, and adapting this to ingredients available in England. She is also keenly interested in the 'why' of cooking, in Chinese medicine, and in nutrition. The almond drink in this recipe is good for throat problems, and is generally energizing and soothing. Drink it hot in winter or chilled in summer.

SERVES 6

90 g/3 oz almonds, blanched
1.1 litres/2 pints water
175 g/6 oz crystallized rock sugar (from oriental grocery
    stores) or unrefined sugar
1 tablespoon bitter almond essence
2 tablespoons cornflour
vanilla extract (optional)

Boil the almonds in one-third of the water until they are soft. Liquidize until smooth. Make a syrup by boiling the sugar in the remaining water for 10–15 minutes, then add the liquidized almonds and the bitter almond essence and simmer, stirring, for another 5 minutes. Mix the cornflour with 3–4 tablespoons of cold water until smooth, then blend into the hot liquid. Add vanilla extract to taste and serve or allow to cool.

BRAZIL NUTS

(*Bertholletia excelsa*)

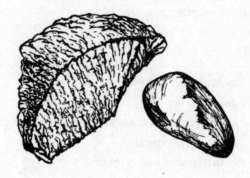

B RAZIL NUTS grow in the crown of one of the tallest trees in the Brazilian rain-forest. *Bertholletia excelsa* flowers 120–130 feet from the ground, then 14 months later produces a large round hard-shelled fruit containing between 10 and 25 seeds, packed together like the segments of an orange and separated from one another by the flat-sided, triangular, woody coverings which are familiar to us as the shells of ready-gathered Brazil nuts. Between January and March these heavy fruit detach themselves and crash to the ground, occasionally injuring or killing the gatherers with their impact. If not retrieved for sale, the fruit are gnawed into and eventually distributed by a rodent, *agouti*.

Brazil nuts have a sweet, phlegmy taste and a high (68.2 g per 100 g) oil content, which yields a good cooking oil (little used, however, outside South America). This oil consists of just under a quarter (16.4 g) saturated fat, just over one-third (23 g) polyunsaturated fat, and just over two-fifths (25.8 g) mono-unsaturated fat. Of our dozen different kinds of nuts, Brazil nuts contain the largest amount of saturated fat after coconuts, and a moderate to high proportion of saturated to unsaturated fats in comparison with all other nuts except coconuts. Much used in confectionery, they often appear, chocolate-covered, in boxes of chocolates, although to my mind they are much more delicious in cakes, where they rarely appear.

Brazil nuts have been imported into Britain as a delicacy since the 1830s. A close, friendly trading relationship grew up between Britain and the newly independent Brazil, which had been helped to gain its independence from Portugal in the early 1820s by the Scottish commander of its navy, Thomas Cochrane (later 10th Earl of Dundonald), the recent self-styled liberator of Chile and Peru. Although a minor crop in comparison with Brazil's great exports, coffee, cotton, and tobacco, the triangular, succulent, dark-shelled nuts, together with walnuts, hazelnuts, and almonds, have long made up the traditional blend of mixed nuts which are inseparable from the British Christmas. Few British people, however, seem to have attempted cooking with them, perhaps regarding them as enough of an indulgence eaten raw.

Warm Salad of Brazil Nuts, Avocados, Parsnips, and Bacon

B RAZIL NUTS and avocado pears, both of Latin American origin, have in common a buttery blandness of taste, which in this dish complements the crispness of fried bacon and the chewy sweetness of a very English delicacy, roast parsnips. A mildly garlicky, fresh tomato sauce unites the hot and cold elements in this salad or *chaud-froid*. An excellent, impromptu lunch dish to serve with home-made bread and perhaps a watercress salad.

SERVES 4

450 g/1 lb parsnips, peeled and sliced lengthways
5–6 tablespoons sunflower oil
450 g/1 lb well-flavoured tomatoes, skinned and roughly
    chopped
3 garlic cloves, crushed
sea salt
freshly ground black pepper
Demerara sugar to taste
6 rashers unsmoked back bacon, fat removed
150 g/5 oz (shelled weight) Brazil nuts, chopped into quarters
4 small ripe Hass avocado pears, halved, stoned and skinned

Three-quarters of an hour before you intend to eat, set the oven to
200°C/400°F, Gas mark 6, to roast the parsnips. Parboil these for
2–3 minutes in lightly salted water, drain them well, then spread
them out in a pre-heated tin, turning them in 3 tablespoons of oil,
and roast them for 30 minutes until they are golden and sticky.

After 20 minutes, heat 1–2 tablespoons of oil in a heavy-
bottomed pan (including, if you like, any surplus oil from the
parsnips). Add the tomatoes, garlic, sea salt, freshly ground black
pepper, and sugar to taste, and cook for 5–10 minutes over a
moderate heat, breaking up the tomatoes with a wooden spatula.
Fry the bacon in another tablespoon of oil until just crisp. Briefly
sauté the chopped nuts with the bacon, then drain together on
kitchen paper.

Arrange the avocado pear halves in the bottom of a dish. Add
the bacon and Brazil nuts, cover with the roast parsnips, and top
with the tomato sauce. Serve at once.

Brazil Nut Potato Cake

A N ENRICHED and crunchy version of soufflé potatoes, excellent on its own with mild cheese and a salad or as an enlivening accompaniment to fish.

SERVES 3

450 g/1 lb potatoes, scrubbed and quartered
2 eggs, separated
2 tablespoons milk
60 g/2 oz crumbly cheese, e.g. Wensleydale, Stilton
sea salt
freshly ground black pepper
90 g/3 oz shelled Brazil nuts, roughly ground or finely
    chopped

Boil the potoates in their skins in lightly salted water until they are just cooked. Drain, and remove the skins if you object to them. Set the oven to 200°C/400°F, Gas mark 6. Mash the potatoes with the egg yolks, milk, and cheese, add sea salt and freshly ground black pepper, and stir in the Brazil nuts. Whisk the whites until they are stiff, fold into the mixture, turn this out into an oiled ovenproof dish and bake for 15–20 minutes until the top and sides are brown and crumbly.

Butterscotch Brazil Nut Cake

I F YOU ENJOY Brazil nuts, you will probably find this generously nutty cake compulsive eating. Light yet rich, with Brazil nut chunks scattered thickly through it, it is best as a flattish, square cake, of the kind which you might take on a picnic or divide into smaller squares to go into a lunch-box.

SERVES 6–8

120 g/4 oz butter
175 g/6 oz Demerara sugar
4 heaped tablespoons/175 g Greek-style yoghurt
120 g/4 oz plain wholemeal flour
1 teaspoon baking powder
200 g/7 oz Brazil nuts, roughly chopped
4 eggs, separated
zest of 1 lemon (optional)

Melt the butter in a saucepan, add the sugar, and cook gently for a minute or two, stirring well. Add the yoghurt, lower the heat to simmering point, and stir until you have a smooth, butterscotch-flavoured sauce. Remove from the heat, beat in the flour and baking powder, then add the Brazil nuts, the beaten egg yolks and the lemon zest. Preheat the oven to 200°C/400°F, Gas mark 6. Beat the egg whites until stiff and fold into the mixture, then spoon this into a shallow lined and greased tin about 20 cm/8 in square. Bake for 10–15 minutes, then lower the heat to 180°C/350°F, Gas mark 4, cover the cake with foil or greaseproof paper to prevent undue browning, and continue baking for another 30–40 minutes until the top of the cake is a rich shiny golden-brown and a fork inserted into the centre comes out cleanly.

Brazil Nut and Raisin Cake

A SIMPLE, delicious Brazil nut cake, which needs no additional
spicing or dressing up to distract from the pleasant texture
and pronounced yet bland flavour of the Brazil nuts.

SERVES 5–6

90 g/3 oz wholemeal flour
90 g/3 oz strong white flour
1 teaspoon baking powder
90 g/3 oz butter
90 g/3 oz soft brown sugar
100 g/3½ oz (shelled weight) Brazil nuts, chopped
60 g/2 oz raisins
2 heaped teaspoons Greek-style yoghurt
2 eggs, separated

Pre-heat the oven to 200°C/400°F, Gas mark 6. Combine the flours
and baking powder in a bowl and rub in the butter until the
mixture has the consistency of fine crumbs. Stir in the sugar, nuts,
raisins, and yoghurt, then the lightly beaten egg yolks. Whisk the
egg whites until they stand in peaks, then gradually fold into the
mixture until this is quite loose. Spoon it out into a round oiled
cake tin, smooth down, and bake for 40 minutes until lightly
browned, then turn out on to a rack to cool. This cake has a good
consistency, and is pleasant when still slightly warm.

Brazil Nut, Brandy, and Orange Butter

TRADITIONAL English brandy butter, melting glutinously over a slice of rich Christmas pudding, or eaten cold in teaspoonfuls from the fridge or larder, is one of those heavy, high-cholesterol treats which often lose their magic once childhood is over. Looked at objectively, a lump of sweetened, alcoholized butter is not the most sensible ending to a large, high-protein meal, while brandy margarine seems too horrible to contemplate. This nutty alternative is excellent provided that the nuts are fresh, and has the advantage that ground nuts, with their absorbent texture, are much easier than butter to combine with brandy. Nor do you have to eat it only with Christmas pudding. It is delicious mixed with a little whipped cream and served in a small mound with slices of freshly peeled orange.

SERVES 4–6

150 g/5 oz (shelled weight) Brazil nuts, ground
2 tablespoons thick honey
2 tablespoons freshly squeezed orange juice
3–4 tablespoons brandy
sweetened whipping cream (optional)

Empty the nuts into a bowl and combine with the other ingredients. If you have whipped cream available, fold in two or three tablespoons of this, and add an extra tablespoon of brandy if the taste demands it.

CASHEWS

(*Anacardium occidentale*)

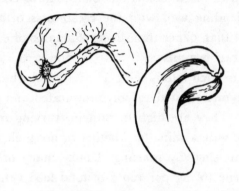

H AD CASHEWS been available in their present form in Europe in the later Middle Ages, they might well have displaced almonds from favour with high-class cooks for their blandness, sweetness, whiteness, and skinlessness, and for the ease with which they can be reduced to a crumbly paste. Try substituting cashews for almonds in traditional recipes (for example, for macaroons, as on pp. 80–1) and you will see what I mean.

Cashews are a relatively recent import into Britain, although they have been known as a tropical fruit to British botanists and explorers since the beginning of the eighteenth century. The English name, like the French *acajou*, is taken from the Brazilian *acajoba*. Originating in the West Indies, cashews were naturalized commercially in Brazil, and then (like chilli peppers, or, in the reverse direction, ginger) transplanted across the world to southern India and parts of South-East Asia, where they are eaten raw, in sweet dishes, spiced and fried as a relish, or in spicy combinations with chicken.

Cashews are the fruits of *Anacardium*, and each hang, in a leathery-skinned, greyish pod with a dark, bitter-tasting layer immediately inside it, from a fleshy swelling of the stalk known as the cashew 'apple', which is fermented and distilled to make a spirit in Brazil and the West Indies. Thoroughly processed at source, cashews arrive in the shops ready for immediate use, either whole or in cheaper, broken pieces. Roasted, salted cashews are often sold as an accompaniment to drinks; but raw cashews have many possibilities, from soups and sauces to biscuits and muesli (in which, blending well with the creaminess of oats, they are infinitely nicer than paper-thin slivers of almond or economical but bitter-tasting raw peanuts).

Cashews are rich in oil, being 48.2% fat, of which the proportions of mono-unsaturated to polyunsaturated and saturated are roughly 9:3:3. They are high in protein, varying from 17.7 g to 20.5 g per 100 g depending on whether or not their water content has been diminished by roasting. Unlike many other nuts they contain carotene (6 mg per 100 g of total food values), but only small amounts of the B vitamins and Vitamin E.

Purée of Young Broad Beans, Basil, and Cashews

E ARLY JULY is the time for tender young broad beans, ready to be flavoured with the basil which is in full leaf in a pot on the kitchen windowsill. If you can grow your own broad beans, they should be ready to pick now: the pods still taut, the little beans covered in a delicate, grey-green skin which bursts after a minute or so in boiling water to reveal the bright green flesh within. When the skin has cracked, drain the beans at once. They are ready to eat. Plainly boiled, with pasta, ham, and a Parmesan and cream cheese sauce; cold, with oil, lemon juice, and a touch of garlic; or in this creamy, light green purée, which combines the young beans with some of the essentials of pesto (garlic, basil, and cashews rather than the traditional, similarly textured pine nuts), but omits the strident presence of the olive oil and Parmesan.

SERVES 4 AS A STARTER OR SIDE DISH

---

340 g/12 oz (shelled weight) fresh young broad beans
100 g/3½ oz cashews, ground until just mealy
2 cloves garlic, peeled and crushed
2 tablespoons torn-up basil leaves
2 tablespoons *crème fraîche*
½ teaspoon sea salt

Briefly boil the beans in enough water to cover with a pinch of sea salt for 1–2 minutes, then drain them and reserve the liquor. Measure 6 tablespoons of this into the blender with the beans and reduce them to a purée. Mix all remaining ingredients with the puréed beans. Heap up the pale green mass in a bowl and serve as a first course, with thin oat biscuits or olive oil bread, or as a summer lunch dish with green salad, ham, olives, cheese, good bread, and sliced tomatoes with basil.

Stir-fried Beef and Cabbage with Cashews

W HOLE IMPORTED cashews cost roughly the same, pound for pound, as good rump steak; and some meat-loving (or meat-tolerant) cooks might find this a sufficient argument for leaving them out of this recipe altogether. They are, however, extremely good in combination with both beef and stir-fried vegetables, giving crunch and a hint of bland sweetness to contrast with the dark, juicy marinade in this variation on a classic Anglo-Chinese dish.

SERVES 4

450 g/1 lb rump steak

For the marinade
4 large cloves garlic, peeled and chopped
15 g/½ oz fresh root ginger, peeled and chopped
1 teaspoon sea salt
2 tablespoons *shoyu* or *tamari* (Japanese-style soy sauce)
2 tablespoons Ginger Juice with Honey (obtainable from
    Culpeper shops) *or* 1 generous tablespoon honey and 15 g/
    ½ oz extra root ginger
1 tablespoon freshly squeezed lemon juice
1 teaspoon Chinese five-spice powder

For the stir-fry
2 onions, peeled
450 g/1 lb white cabbage
6 cloves garlic, peeled
350 g/12 oz basmati rice
700 ml/1¼ pints water
2 teaspoons sea salt

4–5 tablespoons sesame oil
1 15-g/½-oz piece of ginger, peeled and smashed but left whole
225 g/8 oz whole cashews

Several hours before cooking, prepare the marinade. Crush the garlic and ginger together with the sea salt in a mortar and stir in the other ingredients. Beat the meat flat to tenderize it before cutting it into finger-lengths, and immerse these in the marinade. Cover tightly and refrigerate.

About 25 minutes before you expect to eat, chop the onion, cabbage, and garlic for the stir-fry. Put on the rice to boil in the water (if you are measuring the rice in a cup, the volume of water should be a little under double that of the rice). Add 1½ teaspoons of sea salt, bring the rice to the boil, turn down the heat, and simmer, tightly covered, for 15 minutes. Meanwhile heat 2 tablespoons of sesame oil in a wok, and, when it is spitting and almost smoking, add the piece of ginger and the remaining ½ teaspoon of sea salt. Stir-fry the vegetables for up to 5 minutes, until you are satisfied that they are tender and sweet-tasting. ('Wok sweetness' is a quality which needs to be experienced to be understood. If the cabbage is thoroughly cooked and still tastes bitter, this is probably because it is not fresh enough.) Transfer them to a warmed covered casserole or dish; wipe out the wok; replace the ginger in the wok with a tablespoon of sesame oil; and, when this has heated, quickly fry half the meat in it for about a minute, pressing it against the sides of the wok with a spatula and omitting as much of the marinade liquid as you can. Add the tender meat to the vegetables and repeat the process with a further tablespoon of oil and the rest of the meat. When this is cooked, pour in the marinade liquid and stir in the cashew nuts. Transfer meat, nuts, and sauce to the dish of vegetables and seve immediately with the rice.

Chicken with Crispy Cashews

A RECIPE for a spicy, cold snack meal, with potential as party food to serve with non-alcoholic drinks or beer, from Ethel Ow of Munchy Munchy in Oxford.

SERVES 4–5

60 g/2 oz Demerara sugar
3 tablespoons honey
100 ml/4 fl oz water
90 g/3 oz whole cashews
350 ml/12 fl oz sunflower oil for frying
1 medium/small chicken (about 1.2 kg/2 lb 10 oz), boiled or
    roasted and cooled
450 g/1 lb fine pasta (macaroni, angel's hair, or vermicelli)
1½ tablespoons tahini or Chinese sesame paste
1 tablespoon sugar
1 tablespoon sesame oil
1 tablespoon Worcester sauce
½ tablespoon finely chopped spring onion
½ tablespoon peeled and very finely chopped fresh root ginger
½ tablespoon peeled and finely chopped garlic
1 tablespoon hot chilli oil (optional)
1 tablespoon toasted sesame seeds to garnish

Dissolve the sugar and honey in the water and boil uncovered for 5 minutes over a moderate heat to make a thin syrup. Add the cashews and continue boiling for a further 5 minutes, stirring constantly, until the liquid has reduced and coated the cashews. Heat the oil and deep-fry the drained cashews until golden brown, stirring to make sure that they cook evenly. Drain and cool.

Bone the chicken and cut the meat into matchstick-sized strips. Boil and drain the pasta and arrange in the centre of a large serving dish. Combine the remaining ingredients (apart from the garnish) to form a sauce, mix with the chicken, arrange in a layer on top of the pasta, and garnish with sesame seeds. Serve with the cashews in an adjacent bowl.

South Indian Chicken Curry with Cashews

THIS RECIPE is slightly adapted from one included in Mary S. Atwood's *Adventures in Indian Cooking*, a little paperback volume which I have long treasured for its comprehensiveness.

SERVES 4–5

4 tablespoons sunflower oil
1 medium/small chicken (about 1.2 kg/2 lb 10 oz), jointed
1 onion, peeled and finely chopped
1 teaspoon ground coriander seeds
½ teaspoon ground turmeric
½ teaspoon cayenne pepper
½ teaspoon ground cardamom seeds
1 pinch ground cinnamon
1 pinch ground cloves
½ teaspoon grated fresh ginger root
2 cloves garlic, crushed
½ a small green pepper, finely chopped
60 g/2 oz fresh coconut, grated, *or* 1 medium potato, washed and quartered

200 g/7 oz plain yoghurt
250 ml/8 fl oz water
½ teaspoon sea salt
150 g/5 oz whole cashews
1 tablespoon melted butter
juice of 1 lime
fresh mint leaves to garnish

Heat 2½ tablespoons of the oil in a large uncovered frying pan (with a lid) and brown the chicken. Drain, reserve, and keep warm. In the remaining oil, lightly brown the onion. Add the spices, fry gently for a minute, then stir in the ginger and garlic and cook for a minute or two longer. Add the green pepper, the coconut or potato, yoghurt, and water, and season with the sea salt. Stir together, to make an aromatic sauce, then add the chicken pieces, cover, and simmer for about 45 minutes until the chicken is tender. Shortly before serving, quickly fry the cashews in the butter and add to the curry with the lime juice. Serve garnished with mint leaves on a bed of basmati rice.

Curried Lentils with Cashews

A PLAIN RED lentil curry, served on basmati rice or mopped up with home-made *bhatura* (a luxury version of chapattis, made with flour, baking powder, and yoghurt), is one of my favourite vegetarian meals. It can be varied in a number of ways: by adding spinach or a large chopped potato to the lentils for extra smoothness; by using fresh tomatoes instead of tamarind; by serving with chutney or a watercress salad. Reheated, it makes a delicious winter lunch dish with good pork sausages. Here is a vegetarian elaboration, with sweet, bland whole cashew nuts added to the lentils at the end of cooking. This version is lighter with *chappatis* or *bhatura* (see below) than with rice.

SERVES 4

225 g/8 oz red lentils
850 ml/1½ pints water
1 tablespoon sunflower oil
1 onion, peeled and finely chopped
1 chilli pepper, de-seeded and finely chopped
30 g/1 oz dried tamarind
150 ml/5 fl oz boiling water
1 teaspoon cumin seeds
1 teaspoon coriander seeds
seeds from 6–8 cardamom pods
4–6 black peppercorns
3 large cloves garlic
8 g/¼ oz fresh root ginger, peeled and chopped
1 teaspoon sea salt
2 tablespoons Greek-style yoghurt
1 teaspoon butter (optional)
120 g/4 oz whole cashew nuts
fresh coriander to garnish

Rinse the lentils, put them in a large saucepan with the water, bring cautiously to the boil (boiling lentils are inclined to froth over the edge of the pan), lower the heat, cover, and simmer for 30–40 minutes.

Heat the oil in a frying pan and stir in the onion and chilli. Cover, lower the heat to just below moderate, and cook, stirring occasionally, until the onions have begun to brown. Cover the tamarind with the boiling water in a small bowl and infuse for 10–15 minutes. Grind the spices together in a mortar and add to

the onions and chilli; then crush the garlic and ginger together
with a small pinch of sea salt and add these too. Strain on the
tamarind liquid, pushing as much as you can of the tamarind pulp
through the strainer into the sauce. Simmer this for a few minutes
while adding salt, yoghurt, and a little butter to the lentils, then
stir the lentils into the sauce and simmer, uncovered, for 10–15
minutes or until they are of the right consistency to serve. Just
before serving, stir in the cashews and garnish with fresh coriander.

Bhatura

SERVES 4

120 g/4 oz strong brown flour (*or* half strong white + half
   brown)
1 teaspoon baking powder
1 pinch sea salt
60 g/2 oz Greek-style yoghurt
warm water

Place the flour, baking powder, and sea salt in a bowl, add the
yoghurt and mix until you have a consistent ball. If too dry, add a
little warm water. Knead for 5 minutes, cover and leave to stand.
Divide into 12 small balls, roll these out, then flatten them between
the palms until thin, then fry in 1 cm/½ in hot oil until puffed up,
drain, and serve.

Pear and Apple Tart with Cashew Nut Topping

THIS LOVELY tart is at its best in late summer and early autumn, when soft, sweet, perishable varieties of English apple such as Discovery or Worcester need using up quickly, and when juicy pears from England, France, and Italy are in prime condition in the shops. You can make it later in the year, however, using Cox's apples and any pears which feel ripe rather than brick-hard.

Serve as a high-class dessert to round off a light meal (for example, a non-traditional Sunday lunch), or eat as a not too sweet snack at any time of the day. Cashews have a bland texture and a natural sweetness which complement the similar properties of pears, while the layer of sliced apples provides a contrast in both texture and taste. The cashew nut topping seeps down into the tart during baking, merging with the fruit juices to form a particularly delicate and nourishing filling.

SERVES 4–5

---

60 g/2 oz butter

120 g/4 oz strong white flour

30 g/1 oz Demerara sugar (optional)

1–2 tablespoons cold water

450 g/1 lb eating apples (e.g. Discovery, Worcester, Cox's Orange)

120 g/4 oz cashew nut pieces

1 rounded tablespoon honey

2 large egg whites (or 2 tablespoons *crème fraîche*)

450 g/1 lb mellow, juicy pears (e.g. William, Comice)

Make a shortcrust pastry by rubbing the butter into the flour, adding the sugar if you wish, and binding with just enough cold water to make the pastry form a consistent ball. Roll this out thinly and use it to line a 22-cm/8½-in flan dish. Set the oven to 200°C/ 400°F, Gas mark 6. Peel, quarter, and core the apples and cut each quarter into 3–4 slices. Arrange these in concentric circles on the pastry and put the tart in to the oven to bake briskly for 15 minutes while you prepare the rest of the filling. During this time the pastry should begin to crisp and the apples give off a little of their juice.

Grind the cashews in a blender, mix them with the honey, then beat the egg whites until they form peaks and fold them into the mixture until it is smooth and slightly runny. (For a very rich tart you can substitute *crème fraîche* for the egg whites.) Peel, quarter, and core the pears and halve each quarter lengthways. Remove the tart from the oven and arrange the pear-wedges symmetrically, rounded sides upwards, on top of the layer of sliced apples. Spread the topping so that it covers the pears and seeps down into the cavities between the wedges; then return the tart to the oven and continue baking for another 20–25 minutes until it is lightly browned in an elegant pattern of raised streaks. Remove from the oven and cool in the dish, allowing the copious pear-juice to soak away into the crust and infuse the nutty meringue topping. Serve warm or cold.

Cashew Macaroons

THE NATURAL sweetness and delicate flavour of cashews makes them a perfect ingredient for macaroons. These little, light, not too sugar-laden biscuits are quite unlike the heavy, sticky, artificial-tasting 'almond' macaroons or packeted amaretti of the bakery industry, and are my favourite standby for a simple family treat. They are good with mid-morning or after-dinner coffee, and an excellent accompaniment to ice-cream or any creamy dessert.

MAKES 16–22 LITTLE MACAROONS

250 g/9 oz cashew nut pieces, ground in a blender
120 g/4 oz Demerara sugar
2 egg whites, stiffly beaten

Preheat the oven to 180°C/350°F, Gas mark 4. Mix the cashews with the sugar in a bowl, then stir in the egg whites until you have a consistent, slightly stiff mass. Do not be tempted to use up extra, spare egg whites; the cashews must predominate, or the macaroons will be flabby and nasty. Form balls the size of a small egg with wet hands, then halve these with a spatula and flatten out the halves into small discs about 4 cm/1½ in in diameter and 0.5 cm/ ¼ in thick. Place these on well-oiled greaseproof paper or baking parchment on a baking-sheet, or on a well-seasoned tin which has been generously oiled. (If your tin is new, or if you have always kept it assiduously free of a baked-on layer of oil, you will find it easier to peel the macaroons off greaseproof paper than to chip their undersides away from the tin.) Bake for 25–30 minutes until lightly browned, turning the macaroons over with a palette knife after 20 minutes or so.

CHESTNUTS

(*Castanea sativa*)

S WEET CHESTNUT trees are rare enough in Britain for the commoner horse chestnut or conker tree (*Aesculus hippocastanum*) to be referred to regularly as a 'chestnut tree'. Essentially parkland trees, deliberately planted in accordance with a fashion among the rich in the second half of the seventeenth century, they do not grow, as horse chestnuts do, along every other suburban road or in every other moderately large town garden. Sweet chestnuts are particular about their soil, preferring it poor and light to rich, wet, and heavy. Their natural home is in the mountainous regions of Asia Minor and southern Europe, in places such as the chestnut grove in the Lozère where Robert Louis Stevenson slept out with the obdurate Modestine in *Travels with a Donkey*. In many English country-house parks they are reduced by age to twisted, hollow wrecks showing only a handful of long, serrated, shiny leaves and no fruit; but such trees are usually respected for their antiquity, and for the traces of ancient avenues which they reveal.

John Evelyn, in his *Sylva: or a Discourse of Forest Trees* (1664), praised chestnuts as little-known exotics which deserved (in his

view) to be cultivated in England for their usefulness as well as for
their beauty. Naturalized by the Romans in southern Europe from
their original home farther east, probably at the time of Tiberius,
and named after Castanea in Thessaly where they flourished,
chestnuts may originally have been planted in Britain before the
end of the Roman Empire. If so, they no doubt disappointed by
their poor performance in the cold northern climate; and only a
few old chestnut trees, such as the medieval one at Tortworth in
Gloucestershire (said to date from about 1150), were still around
in Evelyn's day, although he quoted a medieval chronicler's
comment that a large chestnut forest had existed to the north of
London at the time of Henry II. It required an optimist to believe,
as Evelyn did, that the trees could produce enough usable fruit in
Britain to nourish the population as he thought they did in the
countries of the south.

> But we give that Fruit to our *Swine* in *England,* which is amongst
> the Delicacies of *Princes* in other Countries; and being of the
> larger *Nut,* is a lusty and Masculine Food for *Rusticks* at all
> times; and of better nourishment for *Husbandmen* than Coal, and
> *rusty Bacon*; yea, or *Beans* to boot, instead of which they boil them
> in *Italy* with their *Bacon*; and in *Virgil's* time, they eat them with
> *Milk* and *Cheese*. The best tables in France and Italy make them
> a *Service*, eating them with *Salt*, in *Wine*, or Juice of *Lemmon* and
> *Sugar*; being first roasted in Embers on the Chaplet . . . In *Italy*
> they also boil them in *Wine,* and then smoke them a little; these
> they call *Anseri* or *Geese*, I know not why: Those of *Piemont* add
> *Fennel, Cinnamon* and *Nutmeg* to their *Wine,* if [cooking them] in
> *Water,* mollify them with the Vapour only; but first they peel
> them. Others Macerate them in *Rose-water*. The *Bread* of the
> *Flower* [flour] is exceedingly Nutritive; 'tis a robust Food, and
> makes Women well complexion'd, as I have read in a good
> Author. They also make *Fritters* of *Chestnut-flower*, which they wet
> with *Rose-water,* and sprinkle with grated *Parmegiano*, and so fry
> them in fresh *Butter*, a Delicate: How we here use them in
> Stew'd-meates, and *Beatille-pies*, our *French-Cooks* teach us . . .

Some of Evelyn's information about Italian ways with chestnuts probably come from Giacomo Castelvetro, an Italian living in England who did his best to publicize the virtues of chestnuts and encourage the English upper classes to cultivate them, as he did a number of Italian fruits and vegetables from which he thought the British might benefit. Nutritionally, Evelyn had been misled about chestnuts; for they provide mainly carbohydrates rather than protein, vitamins, and enriching oils. Fresh chestnuts contain only 2 g protein and 2.7 g of fats per 100 g of all food values, and are not conspicuously rich in vitamins. (The exception is Vitamin C, of which they contain larger quantities than almonds, hazelnuts, or walnuts). The poor who used chestnut flour instead of wheat flour in the mountainous areas of southern Europe evidently did so from necessity, not because this gave them a nutritional advantage; and the rich who ate chestnut sweets or roast chestnut sops-in-wine (sometimes pre-soaked in sugar and freshly squeezed orange juice, as Evelyn advises in his *Acetaria*) did so for pleasure rather than nourishment.

The large number of chestnut recipes for vegetarians in our own century, as shown by the chestnut section in Claire Loewenfeld's *Nuts*, suggests that chestnuts have continued to give an impression of protein-filled healthiness, although comparable quantities of wholemeal bread made with plenty of sunflower oil can be six or seven times as nourishing. No doubt most people eat chestnuts less for sustenance, however, than because they like them, for their natural sweetness, pleasant mealiness, and compatibility with other foods (from sugar and whipped cream, as in the French *Mont Blanc* or *crème de marrons*, to stewed sweet and sour red or stir-fried green cabbage). Even as early as 1600, the French writer Olivier de Serres, in his *Théatre d'Agriculture et Mesnage des Champs*, differentiated between the finest, largest chestnuts, regarded as delicacies and 'known at Lyon as Marrons' (the kind whose size and flavour later made them prized for *marrons glacés*), and the remainder, growing in the poorer areas of the Dauphiné, Haut Provence, part of Languedoc, the Auvergne, the Limousin, and so on, which were the common or garden *chataîgnes* of everyday existence. As a seasonal food for autumn and winter, and material for self-indulgence, chestnuts still have much to be said for them; and on that basis I include several recipes for them here.

Buying Chestnuts

Chestnuts can be found in British greengrocers' shops and super-markets from September until January, or even later. The earliest are the best; and by October prices have usually dropped from the level at which the first, imported chestnuts come on the market. Chestnuts do not store well except when dried, or in the form of purée (which varies in quality from the ambrosial to the frankly dull). By the end of the season you may find that up to half of any chestnuts that you buy turn out to be rotten when peeled; so concentrate your chestnut-cooking activities in October and November, when only about one-third of the weight of unshelled chestnuts that you buy will go to waste in the form of discarded peelings and unusable nuts. For 450 g/1 lb fresh, unshelled chestnuts bought from a good crop in early to mid-autumn, you should end up with about 280–310 g/10–11 oz of usable, peeled chestnuts. Again, for 200 g/7 oz peeled chestnuts, allow 280–340 g/ 10–12 oz of unshelled nuts.

Leek and Chestnut Pudding

UNLIKE MANY other green vegetables, leeks benefit from long, slow cooking in their own juice. Gently braised with chestnuts, they achieve a savoury sweetness which combines well with the flavour of sweet-cured back bacon. In days of war-time meat rationing in England, a plain leek-filled version of this pudding was a standard energizing midday dinner dish, presumably assuaging some of the collective longings for the all too rare real thing filled with steak and kidney. Now, perhaps because they take longer than quiches or pies to cook, and because beef suet has undesirable artery-threatening connotations, steamed suet puddings other than Christmas puddings have become very much things of the past except in restaurants consciously specializing in traditional English food. They are, however, a comforting, simple form of food, not particularly heavy unless solid all the way through. Here, then, is a 'healthy' version of a savoury suet pudding, with a light, dry crust which is high in protein and polyunsaturated fat.

SERVES 3–4

675 g/1 ½ lb leeks, cleaned, trimmed, and chopped
3 tablespoons sunflower oil
sea salt
225 g/8 oz (shelled weight) chestnuts, shelled
2 rashers unsmoked back bacon (optional)
175 g/6 oz strong wholemeal flour
1 teaspoon baking powder
90 g/3 oz vegetable suet
freshly ground black pepper
4–5 tablespoons cold water
250 ml/8 fl oz meat or vegetable stock, strong beer, or other
    savoury liquid

If using bacon, divide the leeks in half and put in two separate heavy-bottomed pans, each with half the oil and a small pinch of sea salt. Stir well, cover, and leave to soften over a gentle heat while you remove the fat from the bacon. Put the chestnuts on top of the leeks in one pan to cook in the steam, and mix the bacon, chopped into 8–10 pieces, well into the leeks in the other. If not using bacon, cook all the leeks together with the chestnuts. Cover again and leave to cook gently while you make the pastry.

Combine the flour, baking powder, and suet and rub together until the suet has been absorbed. Season with a little salt and pepper, then gradually mix in the water until the pastry will cohere into a ball. Roll out as thinly as you can on a floured board. Oil a medium-sized (850 ml/1½-pint) pudding basin, then invert it over the pastry and cut out a circle to fit the pudding as a lid. Cut the remaining pastry into two or three sections and line the pudding basin with it. Fill with the bacon, leeks, and chestnuts, and moisten with 3–4 tablespoons of hot stock or warmed beer or stout. (Guinness is the standard liquid for steak and kidney puddings; its bitterness here would contrast with the sweetness of the braised leeks and chestnuts.) Cover with the pastry lid, damp this down at the edges, and cover it with a double thickness of foil or of greaseproof paper tied in place with thread. Stand the basin on an inverted saucer in a pan of boiling water, allowing the water to come half-way up the outside of the basin. Simmer for 1½–1¾ hours. Before serving, remove the outer covering, make a slit in the lid, and pour in another half-cup of heated liquid, since chestnuts cooked in this way can become very dry. Serve from the bowl.

Lentil and Chestnut Casserole

THIS IS A variation on a simple lentil supper dish which I have been making for years. Lentils, chestnuts, parsnips, and green Savoy cabbage are all good autumn food, whether eaten with game or just with one another. Chestnuts and parsnips, especially, bring out one another's natural sweetness, but need other, slightly more bitter accompaniments. You can serve this casserole with cold duck or chicken, or on its own with good bread and butter and a watercress salad. Allow about 2 hours in all for cooking.

SERVES 4

225 g/8 oz brown lentils, soaked for 1 hour then drained
225 g/8 oz (shelled weight) chestnuts
1 large onion, peeled and chopped
1 green pepper, de-seeded and chopped
2 tablespoons olive oil
1 medium parsnip, peeled and chopped
250 g/9 oz Savoy cabbage, chopped
1 teaspoon sea salt
3 tomatoes, peeled and roughly chopped
3 large cloves garlic, crushed in a mortar
1 tablespoon *shoyu* or *tamari* (Japanese-style soy sauce)

Put the lentils in a saucepan and cover them with cold water. Do not add salt at this stage. Bring to the boil, cover, and simmer for 1–1½ hours, stirring occasionally to make sure that they have not dried out.

After about half an hour, prepare the chestnuts. Nick the skin of each one on either side, cover them with water in a saucepan, bring to the boil, and simmer for 10 minutes. When you have skinned the chestnuts (and discarded any bad ones), add them to the lentils, pressing them well in so that they are covered.

Soften the onion and pepper in the olive oil in a heavy, covered casserole over a low to moderate heat. After about 10 minutes add the parsnip, then the cabbage and a little salt. After a further 10 minutes, stir the cabbage round and add the tomatoes and garlic. Continue cooking for 5–10 minutes more, then break up the tomatoes with a wooden spatula and mix them well with the other vegetables. Check that the lentils and chestnuts have absorbed nearly all their water, then add the remaining salt and transfer them to the casserole on top of the vegetables. Cover and continue cooking for another 20–30 minutes, then season the lentils with the *shoyu* or *tamari* and serve.

Chestnut, Spinach, and Carrot Terrine

THIS TERRINE can be served as a dual-purpose dish. A colourful, filling, strongly savoury accompaniment to roast lamb or poultry, roast potatoes, and gravy, it can also appeal to participants in the meal who prefer to eat no meat. For contrast, serve an additional vegetable (cabbage with lamb; roasted strips of red pepper with chicken), and modify the amount of garlic used in accordance with your guests' or family's likes and dislikes. The flavour of roast garlic, delicious when hot, increases notably when the dish is cold. Tinned chestnut purée, blander, smoother in texture, and less sweet than home-cooked chestnuts, is not interesting enough to work well in this recipe. Similarly, frozen spinach should be avoided.

SERVES 3–4

225 g/8 oz (shelled weight) chestnuts
300 ml/10 fl oz water
sea salt
freshly ground black pepper
4–8 large cloves garlic, peeled
1 tablespoon sunflower oil
225 g/8 oz carrots, peeled and roughly chopped

350 g/12 oz spinach, washed and trimmed

1 teaspoon *shoyu* or *tamari* (Japanese-style soy sauce)

If roasting a joint, duck, or chicken, begin preparing the terrine shortly before putting the meat into the oven.

Cover the chestnuts with the water, bring to the boil, cover, and simmer gently for half an hour. When the chestnuts are soft, purée them with the remaining liquid to produce a fairly stiff paste, and season this with sea salt and freshly ground black pepper.

Meanwhile, roast the garlic cloves in the oil in a moderate oven (190°C/375°F, Gas mark 5) for 15–20 minutes, or on a low shelf in a hotter oven for 12–15 minutes. Cover the carrots with lightly salted water, bring to the boil, cover, and cook for 12–15 minutes. Drain, reserving the water, and add the carrots to the garlic and its oil. Return to a low shelf in the oven for a few minutes longer, then purée the carrots, garlic, and oil together, lubricating with a little of the water if necessary (but not enough to make the mixture runny).

Reserve a few spinach leaves, if these are moderately large and not coarsely textured or tattered. Cook the rest of the spinach for a few minutes in a covered pan over a high heat with a pinch of sea salt and the water adhering to its leaves from the last wash. Drain, pressing out all the liquid, and chop.

Line a small loaf-tin with oiled cooking foil, allowing this to overhang the edges on both sides. Line the foil with the uncooked spinach leaves. (Alternatively, if you have a similarly deep, compactly shaped ovenproof dish from which to serve the terrine directly, simply oil this and line it with the spinach.) Arrange layers of chestnut purée, carrot and garlic purée, and chopped spinach, seasoning the spinach with a few drops of *shoyu* or *tamari* for added flavour, and ending with a layer of chestnut purée on top. Enclose with foil, or cover with a spinach leaf, place the terrine in a *bain-marie* containing an inch of water, and bake in the oven at 190°C/375°F, Gas mark 5 for half an hour or a little longer. Before turning out, leave to stand for a few minutes and pour off any surplus liquid.

Chestnut-flour Cake with Cardamom

CHESTNUT FLOUR has a rich brown colour when moistened, a slightly smoky taste, and a natural sweetness. Ironically, in view of the fact that hill- and mountain-dwelling peasants in southern Europe once endured bread or porridge made from it as virtually their only affordable food, it has a certain rarity value in Britain and a delicatessen-shop price to match. Its recommended keeping period is also a short one, since the proportion of oil present in dried chestnuts (5.1 g per 100 g) is more than twice that present in wholemeal flour. You should find, however, that it repays experimentation.

The classic version of this Tuscan cake is made without eggs, sugar, or a raising agent, and is flavoured with rosemary. I have modified the recipe slightly to lighten the cake, and for the rosemary have substituted cardamom, whose fresh, sharp flavour blends well with the smoky taste of chestnut flour.

SERVES 4–5

225 g/8 oz chestnut flour
1 teaspoon baking powder
seeds from 8–10 cardamom pods, crushed
3 tablespoons olive oil
90 g/3 oz raisins

2 eggs, beaten
6 tablespoons water

Set the oven to 210°C/425°F, Gas mark 7. Put the flour, baking powder, and cardamom seeds into a bowl. Make a well in the centre and pour in the olive oil. Rub this well in, then stir in the raisins, the eggs, and finally the water. Mix well, then turn out into an oiled 20-cm/8-in tin and bake for half an hour until the top of the cake is covered in a network of cracks.

When cut, the cake will tend to crumble, since chestnut flour is low in gluten. Eat it warm at tea-time with butter, and drink Lapsang Souchong for a complementary taste.

Chestnut, Chocolate, and Cashew Nut Pudding

A RICH, nutty-textured pudding, constructed on the soufflé principle. Bland, sweet cashews, with their high proportion of (mainly unsaturated) fat and protein, complement the chestnuts, which are low in both those attributes. Serve warm or cold, alone or with whipped cream or *crème fraîche* for a festive treat.

SERVES 5–6

340 g/12 oz tinned chestnut purée
3 tablespoons Greek-style yoghurt
90 g/3 oz butter
150 g/5 oz Demerara sugar

3 tablespoons cocoa

6 tablespoons milk

4 large eggs, separated

175 g/6 oz cashew nut pieces

Set the oven to 200°C/400°F, Gas mark 6. Turn out the chestnut purée into a bowl and mash in the yoghurt. In a heavy saucepan, melt the butter, stir in the sugar and cocoa, add the milk, and bring to the boil, stirring, until you have a foaming chocolate sauce. Beat the egg yolks and add them off the heat, stirring well; then mix in the chestnut purée. Grind the cashew nut pieces in a blender and stir them in. Finally, whisk the egg whites until stiff and fold them gently into the mixture. Spoon this into an oiled 1½ pt soufflé dish or ovenproof bowl, allowing room for the mixture to rise by about one-third without spilling out. Bake for 20–25 minutes in the hot oven, then lower the heat to 180°C/350°F, Gas mark 4, cover the top of the pudding with foil if it seems in danger of blackening, and continue cooking for another 5–10 minutes until a fork or skewer run into the centre of the pudding comes out clean.

Coffee Chestnut Roll

THIS IS A luxurious pudding, well worth making with real chestnuts, coffee, and vanilla. Although time-consuming, it is pleasurable and quite easy to put together; and the end result is a combination of strong, true flavours. I recommend fresh chestnuts in season for their natural sweetness and mealy texture, although tinned chestnut purée makes an acceptable second-best.

SERVES 4

For the roll
200 g/7 oz (shelled weight) chestnuts
300 ml/10 fl oz water
4 eggs, separated
6 tablespoons strong black coffee
60 g/2 oz honey
30 g/1 oz Demerara sugar

For the filling and sauce
½ vanilla pod
90 g/3 oz Demerara sugar
150 ml/5 fl oz water
150 ml/5 fl oz double cream
3–4 tablespoons milk
2 egg yolks

Slit the chestnuts on either side of the shell and cook gently for 10 minutes in boiling water before removing the chestnuts from their shells. Place the shelled chestnuts in a saucepan with the fresh water, bring to the boil, cover and simmer for half an hour.

For the filling, make a vanilla syrup by slitting the half vanilla pod along its entire length. Place it in a small, heavy-bottomed saucepan with the sugar and the water, bring to the boil, and simmer for 20–30 minutes. As the syrup reduces, carefully scrape away the tiny black vanilla seeds which will begin to coat the sides of the pan and stir them back into the liquid. This is a powerful concoction, and can be made more so by scraping all the remaining seeds from the interior of the pod into the syrup. Remove the pod and leave the reduced syrup to cool.

When the chestnuts are cooked, drain them, and remove any inner skins which may have escaped the initial shelling. Set the oven to 190°C/375°F, Gas mark 5. Line a baking sheet with foil to form an oblong about 28 × 25 cm/11 × 10 in, with a depth of 5 cm/2 in, and brush this thoroughly with oil. Blend the chestnuts, egg yolks, coffee, honey, and sugar together in a blender, then gently fold them into the stiffly beaten egg whites. Pour this mixture on to the baking sheet and bake for 15 minutes. Turn out upside-down on to a rack to cool, and gently peel away the foil.

Whip the double cream until stiff, then add between ½ and ⅔ of the cooled syrup and whip again. When the roll is cool, place the rack over a board, spread the vanilla cream over the surface of the roll and quickly fold it in three before transferring it to a dish. Make a sweet, highly flavoured sauce by adding the milk to the remaining vanilla syrup in its saucepan, heating this to boiling point, then lowering the heat and whisking in the two egg yolks, continuing to stir until they have formed a custard. Allow the sauce to cool and serve small quantities of it on individual helpings of the roll, or bulk it out with additional whipped cream.

Chestnut, Chocolate, and Coffee Cream Pudding

A MAGNIFICENTLY rich pudding with a wonderfully thick, smooth texture. I cannot recommend making it with anything but freshly shelled chestnuts cooked in milk, since these have such nourishing sweetness and such pleasant mealiness, and the end result is well worth the effort of preparing them. A late autumn treat, good for banishing tiredness and damp-induced gloom.

SERVES 4–5

200 g/7 oz (shelled weight) chestnuts
300 ml/10 fl oz milk

75 g/2½ oz plain chocolate (ideally 70% cocoa solids)
7–8 tablespoons strong black coffee
120 g/4 oz Demerara or golden granulated sugar
3 egg yolks
284 ml/10 fl oz carton double cream, whipped

Simmer the shelled chestnuts in the milk for 30–40 minutes in a covered pan, adding more milk if they seem in danger of drying out. Break the chocolate into another, heavy-bottomed pan (a small, cast-iron casserole is ideal), and melt it gently into the coffee. Stir in the sugar, then the egg yolks. Continue stirring from time to time, over a very gentle heat, until the egg yolks have thickened the mixture into a dense, strongly flavoured mass. Cool slightly, then liquidize for smoothness with the softened chestnuts and remaining milk. When quite cool, fold in the whipped cream, chill, and serve.

COCONUT

(*Cocos nucifera*)

C OCONUTS, the fruit of the tropical coco palm, are curiously
symbolic of the economic relationship between the nineteenth-century, Western industrialized world and the tropics.
Unimportant as a foodstuff, they came into North America and
Europe chiefly as a source of low-grade oil, and the material of
ropes and a rough, hairy kind of matting. Costing little, however,
to purchase, process and store, and arriving in bulk at the same
time as cheap sugar (whether from West Indian sugar cane or
Central European sugar beet), they gave an incidental boost to
fairground showmen as prizes in coconut shies, and to the down-
market end of the confectionery trade.

For the American novelist Henry James, looking back on his
distant schooldays, one most enduring memory was of visiting a
confectioner's shop for

> small amber-coloured mounds of chopped cocoanut or whatever
> other substance, if a finer there be; profusely, lusciously endued
> and distributed on small tin trays in the manner of haycocks in
> a field. We acquired, we appropriated, we transported, we

enjoyed them, they fairly formed, perhaps, after all, our highest enjoyment; but with consequences to our pockets – and I speak of those other than financial, with an intimacy, a reciprocity of contact at any, or every, personal point, that I lose myself in the thought of.

(*A Small Boy and Others*, 1913)

A hundred years later, in England, the story was much the same as it had been in 1850s New York. Post-war sweet rationing was over; and coconut, together with masses of cheap white sugar, had returned. You could buy it in the form of pink and white bars of coconut ice, coconut macaroons topped with glacé cherries, chocolate-covered bars of aching sweetness, and those little cup-cakes covered with a sprinkling of desiccated coconut and a smear of jam. Most of these now lie compacted in buried layers of childhood memories, to be disinterred only as the rememberer dislodges a coconut shred from between protesting teeth.

Although coconut now has its adult fans among lovers of southern Indian food (in which it is delicious with potatoes, lentils, or in fresh *sambals* or relishes), there is very little that can be said for it nutritionally. It contains only a minimal percentage of protein: 3.2 g per 100 g for fresh coconut; 5.6 g per 100 g, because of the diminished water content, for desiccated; 6.0 g per 100 g for creamed, or less than can usually be found in the equivalent quantity of white flour. It also contains very large amounts of saturated fat, varying from 59.3 per 100 g of all food values in creamed coconut to 31.0 per 100 g in fresh.

In the confectionery market, there are signs that, with American dominance of manufacturing and commodity trading, peanuts are displacing the once-popular coconut as a cheap, nutty-tasting ingredient for chocolate and other candy bars. Children still seem attracted, however, by its moist chewiness and pure whiteness; and there must be few mothers, other than the most dedicated sugar-haters, who have never tried at least once to make coconut macaroons of the kind which so besotted the young Henry James.

Whole coconuts can be found in most fruit and vegetable

shops. Bore two holes in the softest part of the shell, near the top, to drain out the liquid, and pour this through a strainer to eliminate the gritty bits before using it. It can be drunk straight off as a refreshing, sweetish drink, or used as the liquid element in a curry. To open a whole coconut, leave it in a hot oven until the shell cracks. Once opened the coconut should be used up quickly, since the flesh rapidly dries out and becomes uninterestingly hard and grubby. Hence the jets of water which play over slices of coconut for sale as a street snack in southern European towns.

Roast Barbary Duck with Coconut Stuffing

S MALL, FIRM-FLESHED, low-fat Barbary ducks, which for the past few years have been available in many British supermarkets, should tempt those who like to eat duck in Chinese restaurants but have been put off cooking it at home by the size of most available ducks, their expense in relation to the yield of usable meat, and the abundance of their dripping. The time may now come when large fat-draped Aylesbury ducks will disappear and the leaner Barbary ducks will entirely replace them. Duck, when not too fatty, is wonderfully versatile; and the flavour of its dense, brownish meat, edged with unctuous crackling, is more delicate yet more robust than that of chicken. It is especially good with certain green vegetables, such as spinach, fresh *petits pois*, and mangetout peas, and when stuffed with a mixture incorporating chopped nuts such as chestnuts or walnuts.

It may seem odd to suggest a stuffing for duck containing coconut, with its fatty blandness and tropical associations. In fact, however, this oat-based stuffing is light, crumbly, and piquant.

The coconut enhances the flavour of the strongest-tasting ingredients, ginger and lemon zest, and creates a delicious, sharp treat to follow the flavour of each slice of duck. Try it, as an alternative to sage and onion, when you feel adventurous, and you may find it rewarding.

SERVES 4

1 medium-sized Barbary duck

For the stuffing
8 g/¼ oz fresh root ginger, peeled and chopped
2 large cloves garlic, peeled and chopped
small pinch sea salt
120 g/4 oz oat flakes
60 g/2 oz unsweetened desiccated coconut
grated zest of 1 lemon
2 tablespoons hazelnut or other nut oil
1 tablespoon *shoyu* or *tamari* (Japanese-style soy sauce)

Before roasting the duck, rinse the cavity with cold water and check that it has been thoroughly cleaned out. Discard all pads of loose fat, and trim off surplus fat and skin from the tail area. Crush the ginger and garlic together in a mortar with the sea salt. Combine with the other ingredients for the stuffing in a basin, compress them as much as you can, and push them into the cavity of the duck before sealing it with a flap of skin and fastening with a skewer or a short length of thread. Roast the duck at 210°C/425°F, Gas mark 7 for 1¼–1½ hours and serve with rice and vegetables, or with roast potatoes, roast parsnips, and a thick brown gravy made by liquidizing a roast onion, a roast potato, and the drippings from the pan combined with water left over from parboiling the potatoes or cooking green vegetables.

Fresh Coconut and Coriander Chutney

A TRADITIONAL Indian recipe. Fresh chutneys are best eaten at once, but can be kept for up to 24 hours, covered, in a stone or glass jar in a cool place. Do not put in the refrigerator or freeze.

SERVES 4

120 g/4 oz fresh grated coconut
1 small onion, peeled and chopped
1 large clove garlic, peeled and chopped
1–2 bell-shaped green chillies, de-seeded, rinsed, and chopped
1 teaspoon fresh ginger, peeled and finely chopped
$\frac{1}{3}$ teaspoon cumin seeds, ground
$\frac{3}{4}$ teaspoon sea salt
$\frac{1}{2}$ teaspoon Demerara sugar
2 tablespoons fresh coriander leaves
1 tablespoon lemon juice
coconut liquid, water, or plain yoghurt (as needed)

Grind all the ingredients together in a blender. If the mixture is too dry to liquidize properly, add a little coconut liquid, water, or plain yoghurt. Serve with lentil, chicken, or meat curries, or with snacks such as samosas or southern Indian masala dosais (rice- and lentil-flour pancakes filled with a spiced potato mixture).

Coffee, Coconut, and Banana Ice Cream

A SELF-INDULGENT treat for coffee- and coconut-lovers, good for helping to banish winter depression.

SERVES 4–5

3 egg yolks
120 g/4 oz Demerara sugar
5 tablespoons very strong black coffee
90 g/3 oz unsweetened desiccated coconut
1 banana (optional)
175 g/6 oz Greek-style yoghurt
284 ml/10 fl oz carton double or whipping cream, whipped

Place the egg yolks, sugar, and coffee in a bowl over a saucepan of simmering water and beat with a balloon whisk for 5–10 minutes until light and frothy like *zabaglione*. Remove and leave to cool. Blend the coconut, banana (if using), and yoghurt in a liquidizer (or, if you want the coconut to be very fine, grind it first in the liquidizer on its own). Stir this into the frothy egg and coffee mixture, then fold in the whipped cream. Freeze in a covered bowl, enclosed within a plastic bag if the lid does not fit very tightly, for 3–4 hours, stirring thoroughly halfway through the freezing time. Alternatively, freeze in an electric ice-cream maker in the usual way. If set hard, leave to soften outside the refrigerator before serving.

Coconut Macaroons

A USEFUL recipe for hungry, sweet-toothed families.

MAKES 16–20 MACAROONS

3 egg whites
200 g/7 oz unsweetened desiccated coconut
120–150 g/4–5 oz Demerara sugar

Set the oven to 190°C/375°F, Gas mark 5. Beat the egg whites until stiff. Fold in the coconut and sugar and transfer to a saucepan over a low heat. Stir continuously for a minute or two until the ingredients have begun to amalgamate. Compress spoonfuls of the mixture between wet hands to form haystack or pyramid shapes, and place these side by side on a greased baking sheet. Bake for 20 minutes, lowering the heat to 180°C/350°F, Gas mark 4 if the macaroons have browned in the first 10 minutes.

HAZELNUTS

(*Corylus avellana*)

Ye swains, now hasten to the hazel-bank,
Where down yon dale the wildly winding brook
Falls hoarse from steep to steep. In close array,
Fit for the thickets and the tangling shrub,
Ye virgins come. For you their latest song
The woodlands raise; the clustering nuts for you
The lover finds amid the secret shade . . .

THESE LINES were written by a Scot, James Thomson (1700–48), struggling in his twenties to earn a living in the murk of literary London with his pastoral poetical series *The Seasons*. As an evocation of a familiar form of wild food, they might equally well have been written by a Spaniard, a Norwegian, an Austrian, a Russian, or a Turk; for hazels are indigenous to much of northern and southern Europe and Asia Minor, flourishing in hedges, gardens, coppices, and undergrowth, and especially in semi-wild, scrubby woodland country such as Thomson's Scottish borderland. 'Hazel' is derived indirectly, via the ancient Teutonic consonant-change from *k* to *h*, from the Latin name of the genus,

Corylus. The Russian name for a hazelnut means simply 'woodland nut'; while the French *noisette* and Italian *nocciola* mean 'little nut'. In rural Britain gathering hazelnuts was a traditional semi-festive occupation for young people, marking the end of summer (and of private contact between the sexes out of doors), just as maying marked its occasionally chilly beginning. William Cobbett, writing a century after Thomson, remarked wryly that a good crop of hazelnuts in the hedges always meant a good crop of bastards the following year.

Although gathered, like blackberries, from every convenient hedge, hazelnuts in England were generally regarded as a peasant kind of food, fitter for ploughboys to crack between their teeth than for cooks to shell, skin, and grind for cakes, puddings, and biscuits as they did the exotic almond. We have no tradition of rich-tasting hazelnut cakes made with eggs, sugar or honey, and ground-up nuts in lieu of flour, as in the standard Polish hazelnut cake described in Mary Pinińska's *The Polish Kitchen* (1990), or in George Lang's more sophisticated Hungarian roasted hazelnut torte made with bitter chocolate and filled with mocha butter filling (*The Cuisine of Hungary*, 1971, 1985), or Elizabeth David's Périgordine honey and hazelnut cake (*French Country Cooking*, 1951). One reason for this may have been the difficulty of blanching hazelnuts without an oven, at a time when whiteness in foods was prized and when ground almonds contributed most of the delicate whiteness to banquet foods such as creamy soups, sliced solid brawn dishes (leaches), and almond-milk jellies and creams (blancmanges). In the various continental peasant cuisines in which taste almost always counted for more than appearance, imagination triumphed over thrift, and brown foods such as rye bread and buckwheat *kasha* were honoured rather than despised, hazelnuts found a seasonal place in the cook's repertoire alongside other wild foods such as chestnuts and *chanterelles*. To the conventional English mind, however, they remained the food of squirrels and roistering, lower-class youth: romantic in their assocations with nut-brown skin and hair, but too primitive to deserve serious culinary attention.

Now, in September, greengrocers' stalls display Kent cobs, an early maturing form of the nut, still in its light green husk with pale, green-tinged shell and juicy, woody-tasting kernel. These have a nostalgic as well as gastronomic appeal, while their fresh, slightly unripe flavour emphasizes our preference for nuts as close as possible to their natural state. Later, in the weeks before Christmas, when the leaves on the hazels have long since turned a clear greenish-yellow and plastered themselves to the ground, imported filberts, larger than the English kind and some with reddish-tinted shells, take their place beside the Brazil nuts and walnuts in the shops. Nuts for cracking with port, nuts to nibble with chocolates or dessert; but rarely nuts for cooking with. As a nation, in love with solidity, we have traditionally preferred to play safe with flour and suet.

Hazelnuts are sweet, especially when dried and not shrivelled (as they eventually become with age). The flavour of the fully ripe nuts has an earthy robustness, good with coffee and honey in cakes, raw grated carrots in a salad, or oats and lemon zest in a stuffing for chicken. When roasted until golden, they acquire a crunchy texture and a pleasantly bitter taste, so compatible with chocolate that I cannot taste roasted hazelnuts now without a twinge of gastronomic memory-association, evoking the joys of Cadbury's Whole Nut Chocolate when I was a child. Roasted hazelnuts are included in many of the better kinds of crunchy oat cereal (granola); but the unroasted kind, still in their skins, are excellent in ordinary muesli, especially if picked from the hedge in late September with the last of the summer's blackberries. Nutty-tasting hazelnut oil, recommended in Geraldene Holt's *French Country Kitchen* as a dressing for a salad of sweet peppers, gives distinction to many salads, from plain lettuce to celery, carrot, cabbage, and any parboiled diced root vegetables. Vinegar and lemon juice are out of place with this oil, since it lacks the blandness which requires acidulating. Use it sparingly with a light sprinkling of sea salt.

Hazelnuts are moderately high in protein, containing 14.1 g of protein per 100 g of all food values; higher in Vitamin E than other nuts; and high in fat, containing 63.5 g per 100 g of all food values. Most of this fat (50 g per 100 g of all food values, or about 78% of the total fat content) is mono-unsaturated. Like most nuts, hazels are a good source of nutrition low in saturated fats.

Roasting shelled hazelnuts is the most usual method of blanching them. When doing this, spread them out in a tin and put them in a moderate oven, 180°C/350°F, Gas mark 4, for about 15 minutes. Watch them carefully; the skins will begin to flake off in the oven, and when the flesh of the nuts has turned golden it is time to take them out. Do not overheat the oven, since hazelnuts brown very quickly and the dark brown nuts taste unpleasantly bitter and will be uneatable. Pick up handfuls of the nuts and rub them together over a plate or board so that the remaining skins fall away beneath them, then transfer them to a clean plate.

John Evelyn on Hazelnuts

John Evelyn, author of *Sylva* (1664), recommended planting a hazel grove to walk in for pleasure. Large-leaved hazel bushes, if pruned well below their full height and pleached so that they interlace, make an attractive alley or hedge for a flower garden or potager. The whippy stems of hazel also led to their widespread traditional use in 'cut and laid' field hedges, in which the stem is partly cut through when the sap is dormant in winter and bent sideways to send up vertical shoots in spring. In an attempt to popularize the nuts and rescue them from their image of rustic commonness, Evelyn wrote

> . . . of this I have had experience; that *Hasel-nuts*, but the *Filberd* especially, being full ripe, and peeled in *Warm-water*, (as they *Blanch Almonds*), make a *Pudding* very little (if at all) inferior to that of our *Ladies* make of *Almonds*.

Romesco Sauce

THERE ARE many versions of Romesco, the traditional Spanish
sauce of hot and sweet red peppers, tomatoes, garlic, oil,
and vinegar, eaten as a robust accompaniment to seafood, fish,
and game. Some omit nuts altogether, while some include toasted
almonds, others hazelnuts, or a mixture of the two. Some recipes
tell you to fry the ingredients, others to roast them in the oven
before blending them. Elizabeth David's recipe for Lobster
Romesco, in *A Book of Mediterranean Food* (1950), encourages the
use of up to a whole head of garlic, to be roasted, skinned, and
simply pounded together with a roasted chilli pepper and two
roasted tomatoes. I have based my list of ingredients on the more
elaborate one given in *The Food of Spain and Portugal* by Elizabeth
Lambert Ortiz (1989), substituting the earthier-tasting hazelnuts for
toasted almonds. The result is a thick, reddish-orange sauce, by no
means dominated by the chilli, vinegar, or tomatoes which it contains. It can be served as a dip, with baked potatoes, or with fish.

SERVES 4

2 red peppers, halved and de-seeded
4 tablespoons olive oil
1 chilli pepper, de-seeded and chopped
225 g/8 oz tomatoes, skinned and roughly chopped
4–5 large cloves garlic, peeled
60 g/2 oz good bread
60 g/2 oz (shelled weight) hazelnuts, roasted, skinned, and
    ground
2 tablespoons red wine vinegar
½ teaspoon sea salt

Place the peppers under a hot grill and char the skins until they
are ready to peel off. Skin the peppers and cut into broad strips.

Meanwhile heat the oven to 190°C/375°F, Gas mark 5. In a shallow tin in the oven, heat 2 tablespoons of the olive oil, then add the chilli, tomatoes, garlic, and strips of pepper and roast together for 15 minutes. Soak the bread in the remaining oil. Amalgamate the roasted ingredients, bread, nuts, vinegar, and sea salt, and liquidize together until smooth. Serve hot or cold.

Hazelnut and Sorrel Sauce for Pasta

I F YOU HAVE a clump of sharp-tasting sorrel in your garden, you may look for ways to use it, other than in soups and salads, during the months when it is most succulent, between March and June. This solid sauce, served side by side with a fresh tomato sauce seasoned with garlic and herbs, makes a dish of fresh tagliatelle or other pasta into a balanced main course.

SERVES 3–4

120 g/4 oz (shelled weight) hazelnuts
175 g/6 oz sorrel, washed
sea salt
150 g/5 oz curd cheese, Mascarpone, *or* fromage frais
2 teaspoons butter

After roasting the nuts in a medium oven (190°C/375°F, Gas mark 5) for 10–15 minutes and rubbing off the skins, grind about ⅔ of the nuts in a blender and chop the remainder roughly into halves or thirds. Place the sorrel in a saucepan with a small pinch of sea salt, boil it for 3–5 minutes, drain it, and reserve a little of the liquid. Blend the sorrel with the cheese and ground nuts, adding the remaining liquid if this is necessary to free it from the blender. Melt the butter in a saucepan and stir in the cheese and sorrel mixture with the chopped nuts until warmed through. Season with sea salt to taste and serve at once.

Hazelnut and Carrot Soup

H AZELNUTS and carrots are both naturally sweet. In this comforting golden soup, the yoghurt and curry paste both counteract the sweetness. A good light supper with home-made bread, cold roast chicken or duck, and a dish of mangetout peas or salad.

SERVES 4–5

For the vegetable stock
1 large onion, peeled and halved
2 carrots, peeled or scraped
4 sticks celery, scraped and washed
1.1 litres/2 pints water
1 teaspoon sea salt
black peppercorns

For the soup
1 onion, peeled and chopped
3 carrots, peeled and chopped
2 tablespoons hazelnut or sunflower oil
100 g/3½ oz hazelnuts, roast, blanched, and ground

200 g/7 oz Greek-style yoghurt
1 teaspoon mild curry paste
sea salt
freshly ground black pepper

Allow 1–2 hours for the vegetable stock to cook. Strain it and discard the vegetables. Gently soften the onion and carrots for 10–15 minutes in the oil in a heavy, covered pan. Add the stock, bring to the boil, and simmer for half an hour, then cool a little and liquidize. Stir in the hazelnuts, then the yoghurt and curry paste, over a very gentle heat. Season to taste with sea salt and freshly ground black pepper, remove from the heat, and serve.

Salmon with Hazelnut Butter

THE EARTHY, woody tang of hazelnuts gives an extra lift to farmed salmon steaks, transforming them into a filling and well-flavoured dish.

SERVES 4

4 salmon steaks, about 175 g/6 oz each
120 g/4 oz (shelled weight) hazelnuts
juice of a small lemon
60 g/2 oz butter
1–2 teaspoons *shoyu* or *tamari* (Japanese-style soy sauce)
4 tablespoons chopped watercress leaves

Rinse the salmon steaks and arrange them side by side in a shallow, ovenproof dish lined with a sheet of foil twice its length and width, so that the salmon can eventually be enclosed in foil within the dish. Set the oven to 190°C/375°F, Gas mark 5. Grind the hazelnuts. (It is a matter of individual taste whether you prefer to roast and skin them first. I like their sweet, natural taste when unroasted. If shelling the nuts yourself, remove as much as possible of the loose outer skin of the kernel by rubbing or soaking in hot water and drying with kitchen paper.) Add the lemon juice, butter, *shoyu*, and watercress and mix well together until you have a thick paste. Divide this into four portions and insert these into the hollows of the salmon steaks. Wrap the foil into a parcel enclosing the fish and bake for 25 minutes. Serve hot or cold, with a watercress salad and a dish of Pink Fir Apple or other delicate-tasting potatoes.

Roast Chicken with Hazelnut and Oat Stuffing

FOR STUFFING a chicken, I find it more rewarding to use oats than the traditional breadcrumbs. Oats go well with garlic, butter, and chicken juices, and cook with a nutty flavour in stuffing. They are messier to use than breadcrumbs or small cubes of cut-up bread, but less stodgy in texture and more interesting in their eventual taste. (They also go very well with herbs, especially thyme and basil.) The sweet, woody flavour of hazelnuts adds an extra richness to this stuffing, and follows the Middle Eastern (in particular, south Russian and Caucasian) tradition of serving chicken stuffed with nuts or covered with a nut sauce.

SERVES 4

One medium-sized chicken, preferably free-range
90 g/3 oz oat flakes
90 g/3 oz (shelled weight) hazelnuts, ground
1 large clove garlic, peeled and crushed with a little sea salt
zest of 1 lemon
30 g/1 oz butter
1–2 tablespoons sunflower oil (for roasting)

Pre-heat the oven to 210°C/425°F, Gas mark 7. Rinse the inside and outside of the chicken in cold running water, and make sure that it has been thoroughly cleaned. Place the oats, hazelnuts, garlic, and lemon zest in a bowl, rub in the butter, and squeeze the stuffing together into a ball. Place inside the chicken and fasten with a skewer through the legs, or by binding them together with cotton or tape. Heat a tablespoon or two of sunflower oil in a roasting tin, place the chicken on one flank, and after half an hour allow it to rest breast-upwards, before turning it on to the other flank for a final 15–20 minutes. This avoids the problem of undercooked legs, and should give you an evenly cooked chicken, if the bird is medium sized, in a little over an hour. (Test for doneness by pulling away a leg and inserting a skewer. If the juices run pink, cook for a little longer.)

Chicken with Tagliatelle and Yellow Pepper and Hazelnut Sauce

A BRILLIANTLY colourful concoction, in which the blanket of yellow pepper and soured cream sauce, flecked with ground hazelnuts, suggests a rich, turmeric-infused Indian dish. A blander, more lavish version could be made with chicken breasts; but drumsticks are juicier, and so are less likely than boneless chicken meat to dry out in baking.

SERVES 3–4

2 large yellow peppers, halved and de-seeded
6–8 chicken drumsticks, preferably free-range
1 tablespoon sunflower oil
142 ml/5 fl oz carton soured cream
120 g/4 oz hazelnuts, lightly roasted, blanched, and ground
2 large cloves garlic, skinned and crushed in a mortar
sea salt
freshly ground black pepper
250 g/9 oz fresh tagliatelle
30 g/1 oz butter

Place the peppers skin-side up under a hot grill for 10 minutes or until their skins have blistered and wrinkled. Turn them over for a further few minutes to loosen the skin around the edges. Meanwhile pre-heat the oven to 200°C/400°F, Gas mark 6, and lightly fry the drumsticks in the hot oil until their skin is crisp. Place them side by side in a baking dish in the oven and prepare the sauce.

To do this, simply skin the softened pepper halves and place them in a liquidizer goblet with the soured cream, hazelnuts, garlic (it is important that the garlic and hazelnuts should be already crushed and ground, for the sake of texture and of the taste of the garlic), and a seasoning of sea salt and freshly ground black pepper. Liquidize briefly. Remove the drumsticks from the oven, peel off their skin, and cover them with the abundant sauce. Bake for 35–40 minutes, then serve with fresh buttered tagliatelle and a vivid green vegetable such as broccoli.

Stir-fried Vegetables with Hazelnuts and Tofu

A VARIATION on the familiar Chinese dish of stir-fried vegetables and tofu, which, like lentil curry, must be one of the oriental dishes most often cooked by Western vegetarians. Hazelnuts are less odd in this context than one might imagine. Their crunchiness and slightly bitter-sweet taste provide a contrast with both the vegetables and the soft, savoury-tasting tofu, while their presence in the dish adds vital protein, minerals, and vitamins. If not including hazelnuts, try this stir-fry with peanut sauce (see page 131).

SERVES 4

15 g/½ oz ginger root, peeled
3 large cloves garlic, peeled and sliced
sea salt
2 tablespoons dark soy sauce, *shoyu*, or *tamari* (Japanese-style
    soy sauce)
5 tablespoons sesame oil
280 g/10 oz firm tofu, cut into 1-cm/½-in cubes

450 g/1 lb vegetables (spring onion, carrot, cauliflower, red or
 yellow pepper)
280 g/10 oz basmati or brown rice
90 g/3 oz (shelled weight) hazelnuts, roasted, skinned, and
 halved

Crush half the ginger root in a mortar with 2 cloves of garlic and a
small pinch of sea salt. Add the soy sauce, *shoyu*, or *tamari*, and 2
tablespoons of sesame oil. Marinate the tofu in this mixture while
you chop the vegetables finely . If using brown rice, which takes
30–40 minutes, cook the rice in just under twice its volume of
water with a pinch of sea salt. If using basmati rice, simmer for
10–12 minutes until the water has been absorbed, then leave to
stand, covered, for a further 5 minutes.

When the rice is almost ready, heat 1½ tablespoons of sesame
oil in a wok and fry the tofu cubes until all their surfaces are crisp.
Put them in a low oven (130°C/275°F, Gas mark 1) to keep warm,
smash the remaining piece of ginger to break the fibres, and heat
this with a little sea salt in the remaining oil. Fry the vegetables in
this over a high heat for 3–4 minutes, then, if the pan is dry and
the vegetables still seem in need of further softening, turn off the
heat, cover the wok, and leave to stand for 2–3 minutes. Remove
the ginger, add the hazelnuts and tofu with the remaining marinade, stir briefly over a gentle heat, then serve with the rice.

Hazelnut Custard (Savoury)

T HE IDEA of hazelnut custards goes back at least to the first century AD, when the Roman gourmet Apicius included several recipes for them in the collection which has come down to us as *Apicius de Re Coquinaria* ('Apicius on Cookery'). Hazelnuts were readily available in the wild, and, like olive oil, were a useful source of mono-unsaturated fat.

SERVES 3–4

340 g/12 oz field mushrooms, washed and finely chopped

2–3 cloves garlic, crushed in a little sea salt

2 tablespoons sunflower oil

2 teaspoons *shoyu* or *tamari* (Japanese-style soy sauce)

1 large slice good wholemeal bread

120 g/4 oz (shelled weight) hazelnuts, roasted, skinned, and ground

1 tablespoon finely chopped parsley

4 egg yolks and 1 whole egg

575 ml/1 pint milk

sea salt

freshly ground black pepper

Cook the mushrooms gently for 5–10 minutes with the garlic in the oil in a heavy covered pan. Remove from the heat when they have given off their liquid and add the *shoyu* or *tamari*.

Crumble the bread and mix it with the hazelnuts, the parsley, the mushrooms and their liquid. Break the egg and yolks into a basin and remove the threads to save laborious straining later. Beat in the milk, then add the other ingredients and season with a pinch of sea salt and a little freshly ground pepper. Pour into an oiled ovenproof dish and bake for 35–40 minutes at 170°C/325°F, Gas mark 3. Serve warm or at room temperature, with watercress or a fresh tomato sauce for contrast.

Hazelnut Custard (Sweet)

T HIS CUSTARD is made on the same principle as a bread-and-butter pudding, only with toasted ground hazelnuts in place of the squares of bread and butter. Like these, the ground hazelnuts have a tendency to float to the surface, forming a solid layer which sets first with a delicate, more liquid layer of pale custard underneath.

SERVES 4

4 egg yolks and 1 whole egg
575 ml/1 pint milk
200 g/7 oz (shelled weight) hazelnuts, roasted, skinned, and
    ground
60 g/2 oz Demerara sugar
½ teaspoon cinnamon
zest of 1 lemon, grated

Break the egg and yolks into a basin, remove the threads, and beat in the milk. Add the hazelnuts, sugar, cinnamon, and lemon zest, and pour into an oiled ovenproof dish or mould. Bake in a moderate to low oven, 170°C/325°F, Gas mark 3, for 35–40 minutes, or until the bottom layer of custard seems set. It is easy enough to verify this if you use a transparent dish; but, failing that, make a small nick in the set upper layer and press downwards with a spoon. If the custard is not yet set, it will well upwards.

Allow the custard to cool at room temperature before refrigerating and serve chilled. Decorate the top, if you like, with mint leaves or more halved roasted hazelnuts. Do not stir, or the result will be unattractive.

Poppyseed and Hazelnut Cake

Dark, mysterious poppyseed cake has always epitomized for me everything that is romantically attractive about East European *pâtisserie*. Whereas English mince pies, which are constructed on a similar principle, always strike me as being too sweet, syrupy, and raisiny (and, if made with commercial mincemeat, larded in addition with irritating little shavings of suet), the filling of poppyseed cake is suavely nutty-tasting, blackish, and inscrutable. It can be made with the addition of walnuts, raisins, jam, or stewed apple; but the basic filling is composed of ground poppy seeds soaked in warm, sweet milk and then enclosed in a plain or nutty pastry case. I have chosen this version of mine, which I make with hazelnuts, as a thoroughly satisfying one: dry, yet not too dry, and nourishingly nutty throughout.

SERVES 4–5

For the filling
60 g/2 oz poppy seeds
zest of 1 lemon
60 g/2 oz Demerara sugar

280 ml/just under 10 fl oz milk
120 g/4 oz hazelnuts
1 egg yolk
2–3 tablespoons jam (plum, apricot, raspberry)

For the pastry
1 egg white
90 g/3 oz hazelnuts
45 g/1½ oz butter
90 g/3 oz strong white flour
1 tablespoon (or less) cold water

Grind the poppy seeds briefly in a blender. This releases their oil (which belongs to the nutritionally valuable linoleic variety) and the nutty taste associated with it. Grate the lemon zest into the sugar, mix well in, and add the poppy seeds and sugar to the previously warmed milk in a pan. Stir steadily over a low to moderate heat until the dark grey seeds have blended thoroughly with the milk and the mixture has thickened.

Lightly roast and skin all the 200 g/7 oz hazelnuts to be used in this recipe and divide them into two lots before grinding them separately in a blender. Stir 120 g/4 oz into the poppyseed mixture, remove this from the heat, and stir in the egg yolk.

Set the oven to 200°C/400°F, Gas mark 6. To make the unsweetened pastry, which contrasts crisply with the rich filling, whisk the egg white in a fairly large pudding basin and stir in the remaining hazelnuts. In the same bowl, as a separate operation, rub the butter into the flour and moisten with a little cold water until the dough forms a ball. Incorporate the two mixtures lightly together, place on a board, divide in half, and wrap one half in foil to chill briefly in the freezer.

Oil an 18½-cm/7½-in spring-clip pie tin and, with damp hands, press out the other half of the pastry so that it covers the base and rises at least 1 cm/½ in round the edge. Bake this blind for 5–10 minutes until it has begun to harden, then spread it with the jam (this lubricates the filling, which, although runny at this stage, can eventually become quite dry), and pour the poppy seed and hazelnut mixture over it. Lightly roll out the chilled ball of dough into a circle large enough to cover the filling, neaten at the edges, and return the completed cake to the oven for another 20 minutes, turning down the heat to 180°C/350°F, Gas mark 4, ten minutes before the end of cooking. Remove from the oven when lightly browned, cool in the tin, then loosen and turn out on to a rack to finish cooling. Serve upside-down, cut into wedges, with the perfectly flat base as the top of the cake, dusted (if you wish) with icing sugar. This is good as a nourishing snack with Greek-style yoghurt, or on its own as a rich accompaniment to tea or coffee.

Hazelnut, Carrot, and Brazil Nut Cake

THIS COULD be promoted as the ultimate health cake: nutty, moist, inclined to crumble, and full of vitamin and protein. It is richer, more interesting, and of course more expensive to make than the commercial carrot cake with its sickly, lemony white icing which caught on a few years ago as a take-away snack to accompany tea or coffee. The hazelnuts used here should remain untoasted for maximum sweetness.

SERVES 4–6

150 g/5 oz (shelled weight) hazelnuts, ground
90 g/3 oz wholemeal flour
1 teaspoon baking powder
60 g/2 oz butter
1 tablespoon nut oil

90 g/3 oz Demerara sugar
225 g/8 oz carrots, peeled and grated
2 eggs, beaten
30 g/1 oz (shelled weight) Brazil nuts, roughly chopped

Pre-heat the oven to 190°C/375°F, Gas mark 5. Put the hazelnuts into a mixing-bowl with the flour and baking powder. Rub the butter into the flour until it has the consistency of fine breadcrumbs, then gradually incorporate the nuts. Stir in the nut oil, then the sugar and carrots. Make a hollow in the centre, pour in the eggs, and mix all thoroughly together. Add the Brazil nuts and mix again. Spoon into a 20-cm/8-in sponge tin or a small loaf tin which has been well oiled and floured or lined with baking parchment, and bake for 45 minutes, lowering the heat about 15 minutes before the end of cooking.

This cake is good warm from the oven, when the spicy taste of the hazelnuts is at its fullest, or cold as a snack with fruit or yoghurt in the middle of a working day.

Hazelnut Biscuits

A VARIATION on a Spanish recipe. These slightly rugged biscuits, with their very pure true nutty taste, are good on their own or with any kind of creamy pudding.

MAKES 18–20 SMALL BISCUITS

60 g/2 oz butter
120 g/4 oz Demerara sugar
225 g/8 oz (shelled weight) hazelnuts

120 g/4 oz oat flakes
2 tablespoons Greek-style yoghurt

Preheat the oven to 180°C/350°F, Gas mark 4. Melt the butter and sugar together in a heavy saucepan. Grind the nuts and oats up together in a blender, then remove the pan from the heat and stir these in. Add the yoghurt and mix together until you have a not-too-sticky dough. This is not the kind that you can easily roll out flat; so form small balls of the mixture, flatten these out as thinly as you can with one hand on a board sprinkled with a few more oat flakes, and shape them with a cutter to the size that you prefer. Arrange the biscuits side by side in a greased baking tin and bake for about 10 minutes, then turn them over with a palette knife, switch off the oven, and return them to it for a further 10 minutes as it cools.

Hazelnut and Honey Ice Cream

THE STRONG, pure tastes of coffee, honey, and hazelnuts enliven this rugged yet sophisticated ice-cream, which has none of the syrupy blandness and grittily fine texture of many commercially made nut ice-creams.

SERVES 4

100 g/3½ oz hazelnuts, lightly roasted and blanched
120 g/4 oz honey
3 tablespoons hot, strong black coffee

284 ml/10 fl oz carton double or whipping cream
2–3 tablespoons Greek-style yoghurt

Crush the nuts on a board with a rolling-pin until they are roughly broken up but not reduced to a powder. Mix them with the honey (I like to use a thick white slightly crystalline honey), then stir in the coffee and mix until the coffee and honey are blended. Allow to cool. Whip the cream until thick, stir in the coffee, honey, and nuts with some yoghurt to lighten the fattiness of the cream, and empty the mixture into a bowl or plastic container with a well-fitting lid. If the lid does not seal, enclose the whole thing tightly in a plastic bag to exclude all air. Freeze for 4–5 hours at a moderate setting, stirring well every hour to break up the crystals which form on the surface and round the edge.

MACADAMIA NUTS

(*Macadamia ternifolia*)

MACADAMIA NUTS are tropical nuts which originated in the forests of north-eastern Queensland, and are imported into Britain mainly from Australia. They are also grown in various Pacific countries, notably Hawaii. Round, with light brown, glossy, black-speckled shells, the nuts are solid, creamy-yellow, skinless, appealingly bland and sweet in flavour, and hard yet slightly waxy in consistency. This is not surprising, since their fat content, at 77.6 g per 100 g (of which 60.8% is mono-unsaturated and 11.2% saturated), is higher than that of any other nuts described in this book. They are low in protein, at 7.9 g per 100 g, and relatively low in nitrogen, carbohydrates, the B vitamins, and Vitamin E. Macadamia nuts are sometimes used, raw and crushed or grated, to thicken sauces or decorate dishes in Malaysian and Indonesian cooking. Recently they have also become popular as a Westernized snack, either salted or coated in chocolate, which blends deliciously with their bland, crunchy flesh.

Macadamia nuts have beautiful but almost prohibitively thick, hard shells. When buying them unshelled, make sure that you have either a ratchet-type nutcracker or a plumber's wrench, since the ordinary type of nutcracker will make little impression on them unless you are superhumanly strong. To avoid a frustrating and messy shelling session, it is better to spend a little extra and buy them ready shelled in vacuum packs.

Macadamia Chocolate Flat Cakes

A LIGHT, moist, flat kind of nutty chocolate brownie, in which the clean taste and dense, crunchy texture of the nuts are dominant. Compulsive eating.

SERVES 3–4

60 g/2 oz Continental-style bitter chocolate (70% cocoa
   solids)
1 tablespoon water
75 g/2½ oz Demerara sugar
150 g/5 oz (shelled weight) macadamia nuts, finely chopped
3 egg whites, beaten until stiff

Set the oven to 190°C/375°F, Gas mark 5. Break up the chocolate into a saucepan and melt it gently with the water, stirring until smooth. Mix in the sugar and the nuts, then fold in the egg whites. Pour this mixture on to a well-oiled baking sheet and bake for 15 minutes, then turn off the heat and leave for a further 5–10 minutes. Cool in the tin, then cut out into squares or oblongs.

Macadamia Nuts with Lychees, Bananas, and Ginger Cream

F̲OR AN INSTANT tropical taste and a complexity of textures, you can make this dessert using ready-stoned, canned lychees; but if you do so, serve it at once before the cream becomes watery from the residual liquid in the lychees.

SERVES 4–6

30 g/1 oz fresh root ginger, peeled and chopped
75 g/2½ oz Demerara or soft brown sugar
250 ml/8 fl oz water
284 ml/10 fl oz carton whipping cream, whipped
900 g/2 lb fresh lychees, shelled and if possible stoned, *or*
   2 × 450-g/1-lb cans lychees, thoroughly drained
450 g/1 lb bananas, peeled and sliced
60 g/2 oz (shelled weight) macadamia nuts, roughly chopped

To make the ginger cream, place the ginger root and sugar together in a small heavy-bottomed saucepan. Pound them together with the tip of a wooden spoon until the sugar has become soaked with the ginger juice, then cover them with the water, bring this mixture to the boil, and cook it steadily, uncovered, over a medium heat for 20–25 minutes. When the syrup has reduced but is still liquid, strain it. The most effective way of doing this is through a small hand food-mill or *moulin-légumes*, which allows you to press part of the ginger pulp into the syrup, leaving only the toughest fibres behind. Failing that, however, you can use a wooden spoon and a sieve. Leave the syrup to cool, then whisk it into the cream.

Arrange the lychees and banana slices in alternate layers in a bowl. Scatter the macadamia nuts over them, then top with a generous amount of ginger cream.

PEANUTS

(*Arachis hypogaea*)

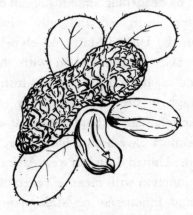

Peanuts are not nuts but legumes like peas, beans, and pulses, the fruit of a pod-bearing plant which grows close to the ground. Originating in South America, peanuts were naturalized by planters in the southern American states (especially Georgia), and in parts of tropical Africa and south-east Asia. Production of peanuts in the United States increased more than eightfold during the first quarter of this century, and by 1925 they had become as much a part of the American way of life as Coca-Cola.

Throughout the country roasted peanuts, which are eaten out of hand, are everywhere sold in confectioners' shops and by street venders; peanuts are also extensively used in making various confections. Since 1900 the food preparation known as peanut butter has become increasingly popular and is now sold by grocers; the value at the factory of the peanut butter produced in 1925 was $6,200,547. The consumption of peanut oil for food and other purposes exceeds the supply available from domestic crops, resulting in extensive importations of peanuts for oil extraction.

Encyclopædia Britannica, 14th edition (1929)

Apart from the enormous growth of the peanut butter industry, the pattern in America has developed much as economists might have predicted not long after the First World War. In 1980, half the peanuts in the United States were sold as peanut butter, 21% roasted and salted and 16.5% in confectionery. Huge quantities of peanuts were therefore being ingested by Americans, nearly all of them accompanied by deadening amounts of salt or sugar. 'Health-food' peanut butter, unsugared and only minimally salted, is widely available in the United States, as elsewhere, but is very much a minority taste in comparison with the bland, simultaneously salted and sugared output of the industrial corporations.

Cheap, very high in protein (25.6 g per 100 g of all food values), and moderately high in both polyunsaturated and mono-unsaturated fat, peanuts have been a life-saving food for the poor everywhere, from the United States to west Africa and the tropical East. Eaten in conjunction with meat or vegetables, as in African groundnut stews and Indonesian or Malaysian sauces for satay chicken, fish, or beef, or *gado-gado* (cooked mixed vegetable salad), they are clearly healthier than in sweetened peanut butter and breakfast cereals, or as highly spiced, thirst-creating 'beer nuts'.

For many years a depressing, if wide, range of choices existed for purchasers of peanuts in the West. There were monstrously over-seasoned, would-be sophisticated dry roasted peanuts; oily, heavily salted, traditionally wet roasted peanuts; and slightly bitter but otherwise flavourless raw peanuts, either shelled or, if unshelled, insultingly labelled 'monkey nuts'. Happily, however, technology and taste between them have now produced unshelled, unseasoned, dry roasted peanuts, which are good to eat plain and can also be used directly after shelling for any kind of sauce requiring roasted peanuts. This removes the need to roast or fry the peanuts at home: always a tricky proceeding, from which they are liable to emerge either flabby or burnt. These peanuts are even good (in my opinion) in muesli, unlike the raw ones which give it a bitter, unpleasant taste.

Peanut Sauce

THIS SAUCE is particularly good, processed fairly smooth, with chunkily stir-fried vegetables, rice, and marinated tofu. (See Stir-fried Vegetables with Hazelnuts and Tofu, p. 115.) It can also be given a rougher texture, for example, for eating with satay-style chicken.

SERVES 4–6

2 tablespoons toasted sesame oil
120 g/4 oz onion, peeled and finely chopped
2 cloves garlic
1 bell-shaped or 2 small chillies, de-seeded and finely chopped
175 g/6 oz (shelled weight) unseasoned roasted peanuts
15 g/½ oz dried tamarind
2 tablespoons dark soy sauce
⅔ teaspoon ground coriander seeds
⅔ teaspoon ground cumin seeds
400 ml/13 fl oz water

Heat the oil in a small heavy pan and gently soften the onion, garlic, and chilli in it, covered, for 5–10 minutes. Grind the peanuts, roughly or finely as you wish, in a liquidizer. Infuse the tamarind in 2–3 tablespoons of boiling water, then strain off the pulpy liquid and discard the tamarind fibres and seeds. For a smooth sauce, put all the ingredients into a liquidizer and blend together; for a rougher-textured one, blend together all the ingredients except the peanuts, then stir these in. Simmer the sauce gently in the pan for 10 minutes, then remove from the heat and leave to stand for another 10 minutes to develop the flavours before serving.

Rabbit in Peanut Sauce (*Conejo con Mani*)

ALBERTO PORTUGHEIS is a concert pianist who finds time, in the midst of a busy international schedule, to create Latin American dishes for his own restaurant, Rhapsody, in Richmond Way, Kensington, and to write regularly on food for the Latin American press in London. The tropical American countries produce a huge and varied quantity of nuts, among them cashews, coconuts, Brazil nuts, and peanuts. As in south-east Asian cooking, nuts are often combined with meat or fish; and Alberto's cooking, which is both traditional and innovative, makes the most of the possible combinations of nuts with other foods. This recipe is Chilean. Alberto points out that Peruvians cook it with a different type of peanut sauce, and Colombians use coconut instead of peanuts. Chicken could be substituted for rabbit.

SERVES 4

4 tablespoons olive or peanut oil
900 g/2 lb rabbit, jointed
2 onions, peeled and finely chopped
2 cloves garlic, peeled and finely chopped
1½ teaspoons paprika
120 g/4 oz (shelled weight) roasted peanuts, ground
1 teaspoon ground cumin seeds
1 tablespoon white wine vinegar
300 ml/10 fl oz dry white wine
300 ml/10 fl oz chicken or vegetable stock
sea salt
freshly ground black pepper
1 teaspoon Demerara sugar (optional)

Heat 3 tablespooons of the oil in a casserole or heavy frying pan, brown the pieces of rabbit, drain them, and keep them warm in a low oven. Clean the pan and gently soften the onion in the remaining oil, covered, for 10–15 minutes. Add the garlic, then almost immediately stir in the paprika and mix well. Return the rabbit pieces to the pan and add the peanuts, cumin, vinegar, wine, and stock. Season with sea salt, freshly ground black pepper, and sugar to taste, cover, and simmer for 50–60 minutes. Serve with rice.

Pork Chops with Peanut Sauce

A RECIPE from Ethel Ow at Munchy Munchy, Oxford.

SERVES 5–6

60 g/2 oz streaky bacon cut into 5-cm/2 in strips
900 g/2 lb pork chops, trimmed of fat
1 onion, peeled and finely chopped
1 large clove garlic, peeled and chopped
1 fresh chilli, de-seeded and chopped (optional)
1 pinch dried marjoram
1 pinch thyme
1 pinch grated nutmeg
450 ml/15 fl oz stock or water
sea salt
freshly ground black pepper
90 g/3 oz (shelled weight) roasted peanuts

Place the bacon in a lightly greased heavy frying pan or cast-iron casserole and fry over a medium heat until the fat runs. Remove the bacon to a warm plate in a low oven and brown the chops on both sides in the bacon fat; then remove the chops to keep warm and quickly soften the onion in the fat, stirring thoroughly so that it does not blacken. Add the garlic and chilli (if using) and fry quickly for a minute, then return the pork chops and bacon to the pan. Add the marjoram, thyme, nutmeg, and stock or water, season with sea salt and freshly ground black pepper to taste, bring to the boil, and simmer, covered, for 40–45 minutes until the chops are tender.

Blend the peanuts in a liquidizer with a cupful of liquid from the dish, and stir this thickening into the rest of the liquid until it coats the pork chops. Discard the bacon if you wish, and serve the chops and sauce with boiled rice or creamed potatoes.

PECANS

(*Carya illinoensis*)

PECANS ARE the fruit of a member of the hickory family of trees with huge elongated compound leaves and brilliant yellow autumn colouring, originating in the Ohio and Mississippi valleys and in parts of Central and South America, and now cultivated in the southern United States. (The name pecan comes from an Algonquin dialect word *paccan*.) The kernels are shaped like elongated flattened walnuts, golden-skinned when ripe, dark brown-skinned when beginning to dry out, with two lobes separated by a hard, papery membrane which should be carefully removed when preparing them for cooking. The nutshell is torpedo-shaped, of a naturally muddy light brown, and cultivated to a greater degree of softness than those of most other nuts. Pecans can be disappointing when bought in the shell from a not particularly fresh consignment, since they can shrink and dry out undetected and are unpleasant to eat in their dried-out state, especially raw. They are reliable on the whole when ready shelled, especially when vacuum-packed.

Even more than peanuts, which were introduced from the tropics into Georgia and other southern states, or the cultivated almonds and walnuts of California, pecans, or hickory nuts, are the true nuts of the middle and southern American states. Mellower and blander at their best than walnuts, they are most familiar, chopped but not ground, in desserts and other sweet things: especially brownies, butter pecan ice-cream, and the classically American, but now anglicized, pecan pie.

Pecans contain a high proportion of fat (70.1 g per 100 g), about three-fifths of which is mono-unsaturated and over a quarter polyunsaturated. This oil content makes them almost instantly convertible into a rich, dark brown butter, which stands out among other nut butters for its relatively sophisticated taste. Simply toast plump shelled pecans in a moderate oven (190°C/375°F, Gas mark 5) for 10–15 minutes, then grind them in a blender, shaking now and then to redistribute the drier, crumblier fragments thrown out by the blades, and their natural oil content will do the rest.

As a source of natural protein and vitamins, pecans do not compare particularly well with other nuts. They contain only 9.2% protein, and small amounts of Vitamin E, the B vitamins, and carotene. They rank highly, however, as an energy food, and blend pleasantly with butter, cream, raisins, apples, and pastry in that borderline region between a stringently healthy and a self-indulgent diet.

Pecans with Bacon, Red Peppers, and Pasta

ALTHOUGH SLIGHTLY dry and characterless when fresh from the shell, pecans combine surprisingly well with some other foods, as in this sauce of bacon, red peppers, tomatoes, and garlic. Their presence in the sauce helps to neutralize the saltiness of the bacon, and creates a nice crunchy texture which sets off the piquancy of the tomatoes and garlic. The sauce is quite filling, and requires only a small amount of pasta to help it down.

SERVES 5–6

2 tablespoons extra-virgin olive oil
2 medium-sized red peppers, de-seeded and chopped
4 large cloves garlic, peeled and sliced
7–8 well-flavoured tomatoes, skinned and roughly chopped
sea salt
freshly ground black pepper
1 teaspoon Demerara sugar (optional)
7–8 rashers thinly cut unsmoked back bacon, cut into thirds
175 g/6 oz (shelled weight) pecans, roughly broken
450 g/1 lb fresh tagliatelle
freshly grated Parmesan

Heat half the oil in a heavy-bottomed pan and gently cook the peppers and garlic in it for 10–15 minutes, keeping them covered with a lid but stirring them occasionally to make sure that they do not brown. Add the tomatoes and seasoning (omitting the sugar if the tomatoes are very well flavoured), raise the heat a little, and cook uncovered for another 5–10 minutes until the tomatoes have begun to disintegrate. Meanwhile fry the bacon pieces in the remaining oil in another heavy pan. Add the pecan pieces to them, stir well, then add the pepper and tomato sauce. Simmer gently, uncovered, while the pasta cooks, then serve the drained and buttered pasta with Parmesan and a helping of the sauce on top.

Avocado, Pecan, and Bacon Salad

A NOTHER INSTANCE in which pecans combine well with bacon, contrasting with the smoothness of the avocado pear. I do not usually dilute hazelnut oil with lemon juice (or vinegar) in a salad dressing, since the taste of the oil is characterful enough on its own; but in this case the sharpness of the juice balances the sweetness of the pecans.

SERVES 4

4 rashers unsmoked back bacon, trimmed of fat and cut in 2-cm/1-in lengths
1½ tablespoons sunflower oil
1 round lettuce, trimmed, washed, drained, and torn
60 g/2 oz watercress or rocket, washed and torn (optional)
120 g/4 oz (shelled weight) pecans, broken into small pieces
2 large avocado pears, de-stoned, peeled, and cut into chunks
1 clove garlic, crushed
1 tablespoon freshly squeezed lemon juice
5–6 tablespoons hazelnut oil
½ teaspoon sea salt
freshly ground black pepper

Fry the bacon quickly in the oil, turning frequently, until it has lightly browned and is beginning to crisp. Drain it on kitchen paper. In a large bowl, combine the lettuce, watercress or rocket (if using), bacon, pecans, and avocado. Mix the garlic with the lemon juice, hazelnut oil, sea salt, and freshly ground black pepper. Pour the dressing over the salad and serve immediately as a simple lunch dish with plenty of good wholemeal bread.

Pecan Pie

P ECAN PIE used to be an all-American treat, rarely seen on this side of the Atlantic. My updated, early 1980s edition of the *Fannie Farmer Cookbook*, America's answer to Mrs Beeton, recommends making it using both sugar and corn syrup (roughly twice the amount of sweetening that I have given in this recipe), double cream instead of milk, and a relatively small quantity of pecans. The result is overwhelmingly sweet, with a faintly nutty aftertaste. Now a cakelike version of pecan pie has arrived on the take-away counters of this country, and, if not quite the true American article, is very much a vehicle for fudgy goo. This more austere version of the pie has a high proportion of pecans to sweetening (2:1, instead of 1:2, as in the *Fannie Farmer* recipe), and incorporates ground pecans into the pastry for a novel and interesting taste.

SERVES 4–5

200 g/7 oz (shelled weight) pecans, halved
150 g/5 oz strong white flour
60 g/2 oz butter
100 g/3½ oz sugar
1–2 tablespoons cold water
1 teaspoon cinnamon
2 eggs, separated
250 ml/8 fl oz milk or Greek-style yoghurt

Pre-heat the oven to 200°C/400°F, Gas mark 6. Grind 120 g/4 oz of the pecans in a blender and divide the ground nuts into two equal portions. To make the pastry, empty the flour into a mixing-bowl, rub in the butter until the pastry has the consistency of fine breadcrumbs, then stir in half the ground pecans and 15 g/½ oz of sugar. Moisten with enough cold water to form the pastry into a ball, roll out thinly, and cut out enough to line a 22-cm/9-in flan dish, keeping the rest for a lattice. Bake blind for 10 minutes, then turn down the oven to 190°C/375°F, Gas mark 5. Meanwhile mix the remaining ground pecans with the remaining sugar, the cinnamon, and the egg yolks. Beat the egg whites stiffly and fold them in, then stir in the milk or yoghurt. Scatter the pecan halves over the pastry, pour on the liquid filling, and bake for 30 minutes in all, removing briefly after 15–20 minutes once the surface of the filling has set to add the lattice. Serve cold, but not chilled.

You can, of course, ignore the lattice and make less pastry or a larger pie; but lattices are relatively easy to make with the right tool, a kind of indented plastic roller like a miniature agricultural implement. Simply roll out a sheet of pastry and push the lattice-making tool firmly back and forth over it until it has penetrated the surface in a close pattern. Tease and stretch the lattice-work apart, then pick it up by the edges and transfer it in one piece to the surface of your pie.

Maple Pecan Parfait

SERVES 4

120 g/4 oz (shelled weight) pecans
300 ml/10 fl oz milk
4 egg yolks
30 g/1 oz Demerara sugar
4 tablespoons maple syrup
2 tablespoons Greek-style yoghurt (optional)
284 ml/10 fl oz carton double or whipping cream, whipped

Toast the pecans for 15 minutes in a pre-heated moderate oven, 180°C/350°F, Gas mark 4. Heat the milk to boiling point, but turn down the heat so that it does not boil. Add the egg yolks and sugar and whisk over a gentle heat until thick. Reserve 30 g/1 oz of the pecans, breaking them into pieces, and put the remaining 90 g/3 oz in a blender. Strain on the custard and liquidize with the nuts. Add the maple syrup, yoghurt (if using), and broken pecan pieces, and fold in the whipped cream. Freeze, either in an ice-cream maker or for 2–3 hours in a tightly covered plastic container, stirring thoroughly at hourly intervals. Serve slightly soft with delicate vanilla-flavoured biscuits.

PINE NUTS

(*Pinus pinea*)

PINE NUTS are the fruit of the stone pine, which flourishes all over southern and south-eastern Europe and in temperate parts of the Middle and Far East, including China. Small and capsule-shaped, they offer less immediate sweetness and crunchy resistance to the teeth than most other nuts do. In countries such as Italy, Spain, Greece, and Turkey, where sweet dishes are usually made with almonds or walnuts, pine nuts have infiltrated the kitchen mainly as adjuncts to cooked vegetables and, especially, rice. In rice-based stuffings for vine leaves, cabbage leaves, and chicken, they provide an element of surprise and nourishing fattiness among the rice grains, being almost indistinguishable from them in size and colour, but melting into sudden oily blandness when bitten into. In Catalonia they are mixed with spinach and raisins for contrasts in taste, texture, and colour. In Italy, pounded in pesto, they all but lose their delicate flavour to the harshness of basil, garlic, olive oil, and Parmesan, while providing the necessary background of blandness and oily mealiness to marry these other ingredients together.

Pine nuts are a moderate source of protein, containing 14 g per

100 g of total food values; a moderate source of Vitamin E, containing 13.65 g per 100 g; and an excellent source of fat, containing 68.6 g of fat per 100 g, of which 41.1 g is polyunsaturated. This makes them second only to walnuts and sunflower seeds for richness in polyunsaturated fat. They are delicate in combination with the less sweet root vegetables, in purées or confits of parsnips, celeriac, or red onion, and blandly creamy in custards, semolina *halva*, and rice puddings. The high oil content of pine nuts means that they burn very easily; so, despite their usefulness as a crunchy topping, do not try to grill them or they will blacken instantly.

Red Onion Confit with Pine Nuts

THIS JEWEL-LIKE dark purple confit makes an excellent accompaniment to the Hazelnut Romesco Sauce on page 108. It is also good eaten cold, like a fresh chutney, with a bread, cheese, and salad lunch.

SERVES 4

450 g/1 lb red onions, peeled and finely sliced
2 tablespoons olive oil
½ teaspoon sea salt
freshly ground black pepper
½ teaspoon brown sugar
60 g/2 oz pine nuts
fresh parsley to garnish

Cook the onions gently in the oil for 30–40 minutes, stirring them occasionally, in a heavy covered pan. It is essential that they should be sliced, not chopped, and that the slices should be very thin. By the end of this time they should be reduced almost to a purée. Season with sea salt, freshly ground black pepper, and sugar. Lightly crush the pine nuts by hand in a mortar or in a bowl using one end of a rolling pin (a blender would reduce them at once to too fine a powder), and mix them with the onion confit. Turn this out into a bowl and decorate with chopped parsley or with a few whole pine nuts for a garnish.

White Fish Pie with Pine Nuts and Broccoli

A LUXURIOUSLY crunchy version of a simple fish pie. I have tried it with a smooth-textured, shellfish-flavoured New Zealand fish called roughy; but it would work well using almost any chunky white fish with a reasonably delicate taste, such as halibut, Greenland halibut, or New Zealand hoki.

SERVES 3–4

500 g/1 lb 2 oz firm, delicate-tasting, fresh white fish
575 ml/1 pint milk
450 g/1 lb floury potatoes, e.g King Edwards, washed and
    quartered
sea salt
30 g/1 oz butter
30 g/1 oz flour
30 g/1 oz freshly grated Parmesan

freshly ground black pepper
100 g/3½ oz pine nuts
340 g/12 oz broccoli

Set the oven to 190°C/375°F, Gas mark 5. Place the fish in an ovenproof dish, cover it with 380 ml/13 fl oz of the milk, and bake it for 15–20 minutes. (Frozen fish takes 5–10 minutes longer.) Boil the potatoes in their skins until soft with a small pinch of sea salt. Melt the butter in a heavy-bottomed pan, stir in the flour, and gradually add the milk from round the fish to make a sauce. Lower the oven heat to keep the fish just warm, moisten it with additional milk, then use this to thin the sauce if necessary. Remove the sauce from the heat, stir in the Parmesan, flake the fish, then cover this with the sauce. Mash the potato with the remaining milk, season with sea salt and freshly ground black pepper and spread over the pie. Sprinkle the top with the pine nuts and return the pie to the oven for a few minutes before serving with the lightly boiled broccoli.

Pine Nut Risotto

A VARIATION on a Greek dish.

SERVES 4

1 onion, peeled and finely chopped
5 tablespoons olive oil
175 g/6 oz risotto rice
850 ml/1½ pints chicken stock
1 red pepper, de-seeded, washed and chopped
1 aubergine, cubed

1 large clove garlic, crushed with a little sea salt
60 g/2 oz stone-in Calamata or Greek black olives, stoned and
    halved
100 g/3½ oz pine nuts
sea salt
freshly ground black pepper
fresh mint (optional)

Gently soften the onion for 10 minutes in 2 tablespoons of oil in a
heavy, covered pan. Stir in the rice, then add a few tablespoons of
stock and continue stirring until the stock has been absorbed.
Repeat the process, standing over the uncovered pan and raising
or lowering the heat as appropriate, until the process of stirring
and simmering has caused the rice to soften glutinously. This
should take about 15 minutes and use up most or all of the stock.
Meanwhile heat the remaining oil in a frying-pan and fry the
pepper and aubergine until the pepper is soft and the aubergine
crisp. Add the garlic and fry gently for a minute or two longer;
then stir the vegetables into the rice with the olive halves or pieces
and the pine nuts. (I do not recommend the tidier, but more
tastelessly rubbery, pre-stoned olives.) Season and garnish with a
little chopped fresh mint if available and serve at once.

Duck with Pine Nuts

A N ORIENTAL recipe with a Middle Eastern influence, from
Ethel Ow at Munchy Munchy in Oxford. Like walnuts,
which are crushed to a paste and cooked with duck in the Persian
dish *fezanjan*, pine nuts have a pleasant, nutritious oiliness which
blends well with dry, tasty duck meat, and in this recipe thicken

the sauce in which it is braised. It is characteristic of Ethel's style of cooking, and of her Indonesian background, to use nuts for thickening a sauce, taking advantage of the nourishing properties of locally available nuts, rather than using cornflour in the Chinese manner. In Indonesia the thickening might be done with tropical candlenuts (*kemiri*; *buah keras* in Malaysian) or macadamia nuts. In England, Ethel uses almonds, pine nuts, or any other nuts which lend themselves to thickening and suit the particular spicy character of the dish.

SERVES 4

- 1 medium-sized Barbary or other duck, quartered, with skin left on
- 1 onion, peeled and finely chopped
- 2 cloves garlic, peeled and chopped
- 1 teaspoon peeled, crushed and finely chopped fresh ginger
- 1 tablespoon roasted and coarsely mortar-ground coriander seeds
- 1 teaspoon ground cardamom seeds
- ½ teaspoon grated nutmeg
- ½ teaspoon sea salt
- 60 g/2 oz pine nuts, lightly toasted, half crushed to a paste and half left whole
- 1 teaspoon honey
- 400 ml/14 fl oz duck or chicken stock
- 2 tablespoons plain yoghurt
- 2 tablespooons chopped fresh coriander leaves (to garnish)

Heat a well-seasoned wok or large heavy saucepan, put in the duck quarters, and stir them briskly over a moderate to high heat until the skin begins to crisp and the fat to run. Add the onion, garlic, and ginger and continue frying in the duck fat for a further 5 minutes until the onion has softened. Add the spices and sea salt and stir well, then add the crushed pine-nut paste and honey and continue stir-frying for a further minute. Pour on the stock to cover the duck, transfer to a casserole, and cook uncovered in a moderate oven, 180°C/350°F, Gas mark 4, for 40–45 minutes until the duck is tender. If still very liquid, reduce the juices by boiling for a few minutes on the top of the stove, then remove from the heat, stir in the yoghurt until it is dissolved into the sauce, and serve garnished with the remaining pine nuts and chopped coriander leaves.

Apricot and Pine Nut Pudding

A LOVELY PUDDING, consisting of a pine nut custard topped with a layer of baked apricot meringue. Apricots are high in potassium and Vitamin A and B³, so this combination is exceptionally healthful. Great care needs to be taken not to overcook the custard before adding the meringue, or the custard may separate during the last stage of baking.

SERVES 4

4 egg yolks
300 ml/10 fl oz milk
60 g/2 oz Demerara or soft brown sugar
60 g/2 oz pine nuts
250 g/9 oz dried apricots, washed and soaked
2 egg whites, stiffly beaten

Whisk the egg yolks into the milk and remove any obvious threads with a teaspoon. Add the sugar and pine nuts, pour into an ovenproof dish, and bake for 25–30 minutes at 150°C/300°F, Gas mark 2. Meanwhile, cook the soaked apricots until soft in just enough water to cover them, then liquidize them to a purée. Fold in the egg whites and spoon this meringue over the surface of the custard, which should be just beginning to set. Continue baking for another 20–25 minutes, until the meringue is lightly browned and the layer of custard underneath is set. Leave to cool and serve at room temperature.

PISTACHIOS

(*Pistacia vera*)

PISTACHIOS are the fruits of a small tree, originally from Syria, which now flourishes in many Mediterranean areas, in Asia Minor, and the south-western United States. The vivid green of the nuts, separated from their reddish skins, colours ice cream and (in central Europe) cream fillings for *pâtisserie*. They appear embedded in Montélimar nougat, in the oriental sweet *rahat locoum* and the ice-cream cake, *cassata*, of southern Italy and Sicily. In the Middle East and India they are often sold, fried and/or salted, as a relish to eat with drinks. In Britain, too, they are usually sold roasted, and sometimes salted, in their split shells. Once shelled, these can be incorporated in savoury recipes; but it is also possible, in larger supermarkets, to find packets of ready shelled unsalted pistachios to grind or chop for use in sweet dishes.

I fell in love with the idea of pistachio ice cream one June evening in northern Italy. Round and round the ramparts we walked, two eighteen-year-old girls, Franca and I, on an interminable *passeggiata*. Avoiding the routine glances of lonely young soldiers who had been let out of barracks for a few hours in the evening, and who must have wondered why we were there at all if not to be chatted up by them, we maintained a prim outward respectability as we made laboriously polite conversation. Franca worked in a city office, lived at home with her parents, and had been taking English lessons; I was killing time before going to university. Was I engaged at home? No, of course not, I answered perhaps too readily, crushing hopes of a ring, a photograph of the *fidanzato*. As the conversation flagged, we stopped from time to time at the outdoor stalls selling ice cream in what were to me, then, exotic and deliciously genuine flavours: pistachio, *nocciola*, *zabaglione*. Coming from a post-war English childhood of cardboard-wrapped ice-cream bricks artifically flavoured with vanilla, chocolate, or strawberry, I was intrigued by the daring bright green colour and delicate flavour of pistachio, and amazed that one could simply buy it from a barrow on the street. No subsequent tastings have ever had quite the same impact; and the romance of pistachio remains in my memory, against a background of revving motor-scooters and promenading high heels, that summer of Kennedy and Khrushchev, the Profumo scandal, and the end (as it later seemed to many people) of the simple austerities of the post-war era.

The ancient Romans, who loved piquant garnishes to scatter over their food, were fond of pistachios and imported them from Syria into southern Europe. Similar tastes for exotic delicacies prevailed in late eighteenth- and early nineteenth-century England, when pistachios (spelt 'pistatia nutts') could be found in specialist grocery shops such as Ambrose Peck's Italian Warehouse in the Strand, London. But what cooks did with them once they got them home is less well known. There is a recipe for some strikingly greenish pistachio macaroons (4 oz bitter almonds, 12 oz sugar, 6 oz pistachio kernels, 1 tablespoon vanilla, sugar, and 2 stiffly beaten egg whites) in *The Royal Confectioner, English and Foreign* (1874) by Queen Victoria's former chef, Charles Elmé Francatelli. Byron mentions pistachio nuts with lamb as a Near Eastern delicacy; and they were no doubt used, in the England in which he grew up, to colour and flavour the kind of luxurious ice creams which were served only to the rich at grand ball suppers.

Pistachios contain a moderate amount of protein (17.9 g per 100 g when roasted and salted) and a moderate amount of fat (55.4 g per 100 g when roasted and salted; 49.8 g per 100 g when their normal water content is still present). Half this fat is monounsaturated, and just under one-third of it is polyunsaturated. Pistachios are higher in carotene (130 mg per 100 g) than any other nuts considered in this book, and contain small amounts of all the B vitamins. Although rarely eaten in large quantities, they are a valuable source of nutrition, on their own, in soups and solid meat or vegetable dishes (for example, mixed with cooked spinach or in vegetable samosas), or with sweet things.

Cauliflower and Pistachio Soup

Nuts in soup sometimes simply have a thickening effect, or add a mealiness to the texture. Pistachios, however, give a creaminess to this soup, counteracting the slight roughness of the cauliflower and complementing its naturally nutty taste with a stronger, more interesting taste of their own.

SERVES 3–4

- 1 onion, peeled and chopped
- 1 carrot, peeled and chopped
- 2 tablespoons sunflower oil
- ½ medium-sized cauliflower, washed and divided into florets
- 1.1 litres/2 pints good chicken stock, strained, refrigerated, and skimmed
- 60 g/2 oz (shelled weight) pistachio nuts

sea salt
freshly ground black pepper

Gently soften the onion and carrot for 10–15 minutes in the oil in a heavy covered pan. Add the cauliflower florets, stir round well, and continue softening for a further 5–10 minutes. Pour on the stock, bring to the boil, and simmer for half an hour; then add the pistachios, leave to cool for 10–15 minutes, and liquidize. Adjust the seasoning, depending on the amount of sea salt and freshly ground black pepper already added to the stock, and serve warm or cold.

Carrot and Pistachio Salad

REDDISH-BROWN toasted sesame oil with its smoky, nutty scent, faintly reminiscent of the smell of streaky bacon crisping, makes an unfailingly good winter lunchtime dish out of plain grated carrot salad. Do not overdo the dressing; it takes time to sink in, and the grated carrot should not be swimming in it. Sesame oil is also recommended for stir-frying, and is worth having as a standby both for making this salad and for frying any vegetable to which you want to give a strong, characterful taste.

SERVES 4

4 large carrots
4 tablespoons sesame oil
2 teaspoons balsamic vinegar
½ teaspoon sea salt

freshly ground black pepper
60 g/2 oz (shelled weight) pistachios
120 g/4 oz white or Savoy cabbage, finely chopped (optional)

Peel and grate the carrots into a bowl. Stir in the oil, vinegar, sea salt, and freshly ground black pepper. Arrange in a mound in the centre of a plate or dish and scatter the pistachios on top. If you wish, surround this colourful green-and-orange salad with a ring of finely chopped Savoy or white cabbage. Kent cobs or filberts, milkily sweet and fresh in the shell in late September and early October, hazelnuts, or walnuts would do well as a substitute for pistachios.

Aubergine and Pistachio Gratin

A UBERGINES baked with Mozzarella are a traditional Apulian dish from southern Italy. This is a more substantial and protein-filled version, good as a light supper dish with a home-made vegetable soup, or with baked potatoes and another hot vegetable such as spinach or grilled tomatoes.

SERVES 3

1 large aubergine, about 400 g/14 oz in weight
8–10 tablespoons olive oil
100 g/3½ oz (shelled weight) pistachios, ground
2 large cloves garlic, peeled, and crushed in a mortar
175 g/6 oz Ricotta cheese

sea salt
freshly ground black pepper
150 g/5 oz Mozzarella

Slice the aubergine and halve all but the smallest slices. Fry these in batches in olive oil over a moderate heat in a covered pan until soft and lightly browned and crisped. You will find that the first batch needs several tablespoons of oil, but that subsequent batches need less as they absorb the oily residue left in the pan. Drain on absorbent kitchen paper and arrange side by side in a large shallow ovenproof dish. Set the oven to 200°C/400°F, Gas mark 6.

Meanwhile, mix the pistachios and the garlic with the Ricotta and season with sea salt and freshly ground black pepper. Spread this mixture over the aubergines and cover with thin slices of Mozzarella. Bake for 20 minutes, pour off any surplus liquid from round the edge of the dish, and serve. For a crisper finish, the aubergine slices may be rolled in ground pistachios on both sides before baking.

Lamb with Pistachios

I WAS PROMPTED to try this idea by Byron's account in *Don Juan* of a dinner given by the beautiful Greek girl, Haidée, to her lover.

> The dinner made about a hundred dishes;
> Lamb and pistachio nuts – in short, all meats,
> And saffron soups, and sweetbreads; and the fishes
> Were of the finest that e'er flounced in nets,
> Drest to a Sybarite's most pamper'd wishes . . .

Lamb and pistachio nuts. The phrase pursued me until I half-believed that I had seen it in the index to a cookery book; but, searching for this enticing combination, I found nothing. Probably, I realized, the dish that Byron meant was a ragoût with nuts added at the end of cooking, since spit-roasting would have been difficult to combine with the use of pistachios. Here, however, I have made the pistachios into a crust for roasting lamb, moistened with Greek yoghurt and flavoured with garlic. The strongly savoury taste of pistachios gives an extra relish to the meat juice which soaks into the crust, keeping the meat underneath it succulently juicy.

SERVES 4

120 g/4 oz roasted pistachios in the shell (or 60 g/2 oz shelled)
2–3 large cloves garlic, peeled
1 pinch sea salt
2 heaped tablespoons Greek-style yoghurt
1 1–1.5 kg/2–3 lb half-leg of lamb (knuckle or fillet end)
3 tablespoons olive oil for roasting
1 kg/2 lb 3 oz roasting potatoes, e.g. King Edwards, scrubbed, halved or quartered
1–2 onions

Shell the pistachios. As you do so they will split in two, revealing a bright green interior. Discard any which are yellow or shrunken, and rub the rest together to shed as much as possible of their dark brown papery skins. Grind in a blender. Roasted pistachios are dry and will form a loose, green, mealy substance. Crush one of the garlic cloves in a mortar with a little sea salt, add the yoghurt, then mix in the pistachios until you have a light paste. Cut the remaining garlic clove(s) into slivers and insert these into slits made with a knife-point in the lean meat of the lamb. Trim off all fat from the lamb, exposing the lean meat around the edges.

Preheat the oven to 230°C/450°F, Gas mark 8. Heat the oil in a large roasting-tin. Parboil for 5 minutes any potatoes which you may be roasting, drain, conserving the water for gravy, and arrange the potatoes and onions round the edge of the tin. Place the lamb in the centre and spoon on the pistachio paste so that it covers all the exposed lean meat and part of the remaining skin. If you have a knuckle rather than a fillet end of lamb, the paste on the vertical surface will be inclined to slip down to the bottom of the pan as it absorbs more of the juices. Check on this every now and then, and spoon up on to the top of the joint any paste which has become detached from it. Press the paste well down.

Roast for 1 hour to 1 hour and 25 minutes depending on the size of the joint (25 minutes + 20 minutes per lb). After roasting, make gravy by deglazing the pan juices with water from the potatoes or vegetables, and liquidizing this with the roast onion(s), a roast potato or two, and a little sea salt and pepper. This liquid should be a delicious rich brown colour. Carve the joint in medallions or chunks rather than in slices in order to share out fairly the juice-saturated pistachio paste. Serve with cauliflower or broccoli, roast potatoes, and gravy.

Semolina, Pistachio, and Lime Cream

A BRILLIANTLY white, cold, creamy pudding, beautiful to look at, with a satisfying, nutty solidity. It is a lighter, Westernized derivative of the various Middle Eastern and south-east European versions of semolina pudding, known as *halva*, *halawa*, or *ma'mounia*, in which semolina is cooked in butter, then mixed with lemon juice or nuts and a sugar syrup. For the original versions, see Lesley Chamberlain, *The Food and Cooking of Eastern Europe*, pp. 427–8, and Claudia Roden, *A Book of Middle Eastern Food*, p. 401. If you find the flavour of pistachios and honey in this pudding too delicate, add the crushed seeds of two cardamom pods to the semolina before mixing this with the liquid ingredients.

SERVES 6–8

75 g/2½ oz butter
150 g/5 oz Demerara sugar
300 ml/10 fl oz milk
250 g/9 oz semolina
3 tablespoons Greek-style yoghurt
175 g/6 oz (shelled weight) unsalted pistachio nuts, roasted
    and roughly chopped
juice of 2 squeezed limes
2 tablespoons honey
284 ml/10 fl oz carton whipping cream, whipped
crystallized lime or angelica pieces to decorate (optional)

Melt the butter in a heavy-bottomed saucepan, stir in the sugar, then add the milk and bring to the boil to form a foaming, butterscotch liquid. Stir in the semolina, which will immediately absorb the liquid, then lower the heat and add the yoghurt. Beat well over a gentle heat for 2–3 minutes until light and fluffy, then remove from the heat and stir in the nuts and lime juice. Leave to stand and cool for 10 minutes while you whip the cream, add the honey to it, and whip again until stiff. Fold the cream gently into the semolina mixture, turn out into a dish, cover with clingfilm, and refrigerate overnight or for several hours before serving. Decorate, if you wish, with crystallized lime or angelica.

Pistachio Cream Cake

T HIS SOLID, greenish-golden cake is good to eat on its own as a nourishing snack, or would make a grand dessert piled high with vanilla cream, preserved peaches or pears drained of their liquid, and a scattering of pistachios and whole blanched almonds.

SERVES 4–5

200 g/7 oz (shelled weight) unsalted pistachios, ground
1 rounded tablespoon thick honey
60 g/2 oz Demerara or golden granulated sugar
2 rounded tablespoons Greek-style yoghurt
142 ml/5 fl oz carton double cream, whipped
2 eggs, separated

Mix together the pistachios, honey, sugar, and yoghurt, and fold in the cream. (For a simple topping to the cake or pudding, reserve two tablespoons of ground pistachios, scatter them on a plate, and roll 2–3 tablespoons of the pistachio, cream, and yoghurt mixture in them until it is well coated in powdery green. Keep back this topping until the cake has cooked and cooled.) Set the oven to 190°C/375°F, Gas mark 5. Stir the egg yolks into the mixture, then whisk the whites until stiff and fold them in. If intending to use the cake as a base for dessert, bake it in a shallow, buttered ovenproof dish for 20–25 minutes; otherwise, in a more compact dish or tin for 25–30 minutes, or until cooked through.

WALNUTS

(*Juglans regia*)

BIG GOLDEN-SKINNED Californian walnuts, kiln-dried in their pale buff shells, are a now familiar sight to food shoppers, not only on market stalls before Christmas but in supermarkets most of the year round. These walnuts, although American grown, are almost invariably the improved strains of *Juglans regia*, known in America as the English walnut, rather than the harder-skinned *Juglans nigra* or American black walnut. Their cultivation in California, where they were introduced by Jesuits in the eighteenth century, has boomed in recent years with new processing technology and the growth in demand in both America and Europe for clean, healthy, easily transportable forms of food.

Unlike almonds, the other great Californian nut crop, walnuts are too oily and difficult to skin to respond well to being roasted and salted as snacks to eat with drinks. It is this high oil content, consisting mainly of polyunsaturated fat, which makes walnuts such a good ingredient in salads, soups, and cakes. Walnuts have an attractive slight bitterness of taste, varying from very pronounced and fresh in new, wet walnuts to mild and mellow in the finest kiln-dried walnuts, and frankly rancid in that small proportion of ready-shelled walnut halves or pieces which travel too far and are left to sit for too long in warehouses before arriving on supermarket or health-food shop shelves.

It was in California, at Loma Linda University, that recent dietary trials (reported in the *New England Journal of Medicine*, 4 March 1993) found that walnuts were effective in lowering blood cholesterol levels, their ratio of polyunsaturated to saturated fats being 8.5:1, one of the highest naturally occurring in any form of food. In a six-year study, eighteen healthy men were placed on two four-week-long controlled diets, one of 'normal' American food, the other with one-fifth of the fattier food (meat, oil, margarine, and butter) replaced by raw walnuts. At the end of the period, cholesterol levels in the walnut-eating group were significantly lower than those in the non-walnut eating group. Walnuts are thus clearly a desirable food, however they are eaten; and a big bowl of unshelled new walnuts, with nutcrackers handy, can do more in the long term to satisfy the casual snacking needs of children and adults than all the sugar- and saturated fat-laden content of commercially made biscuits, chocolate, and cakes.

The early Roman and northern European impulse to naturalize walnut trees from their home in south-eastern Europe and Asia Minor suggests an equally early awareness of the health-giving qualities and palatability of the nuts. *Iuglans*, in Latin, means 'Jove's nut', *Iovis glans*, surely the ultimate distinction. In French, Italian, and Spanish the walnut is simply 'the nut': '*le noix*', '*il noce*', '*el nuece*'. Its later arrival in northern Europe can be seen from the alienizing 'wal-' root in English and German which gives us Wales and the many Waltons, full of incomers, on the outskirts of English towns and cities, and which made the walnut the 'foreign nut' or 'Gaul nut'. Its Russian name, '*gretsky orekh*', means 'Greek nut', as distinct from the 'common nut' or 'woodland nut' which grew on the native hazel bushes in Russian forest undergrowth.

By the second half of the seventeenth century, when John Evelyn wrote his *Sylva*, walnut trees were well established throughout most of Europe. They occurred in cornfields, he reported, or along roads or the avenues leading to country houses. In Germany, in the neighbourhood of Hanover and Frankfurt-am-Main, no young farmer was allowed to marry until he could prove that he had planted and nurtured a stated number of walnut trees. Not far away, the thirty-mile Bergstrasse from Heidelberg to Darmstadt was lined with walnut trees, just as, in the 1920s, most of the Czechoslovak walnut crop came from trees planted along the public highways and owned collectively by the villages.

Evelyn was chiefly enthusiastic about the timber produced by walnut trees, which, as a material for furniture and utensils, he considered far superior to beech. His familiarity with the culinary use of whole walnuts seems to have been limited to green walnut pickle, since discovered (with green walnut jam or marmalade) to be a highly concentrated source of Vitamin C. He acknowledged, however, that the Spaniards liked to grate dried walnuts over tarts and other dishes, and that the French enjoyed blanched new walnuts with salt and wine. He also noticed that in parts of France walnut oil was used for frying, that 'they . . . eat it instead of *Butter*, in Berry, where they have little or none good'. Fifteen pounds of shelled nuts, he added, 'will yield half as much *Oyl*, which the sooner 'tis drawn, is the more in quantity, though the dryer the *Nut*, the more in quality'. He seems, however, to have been unaware of the delicious walnut jams or marmalades made with sugar ('most highly prized') or honey ('passably good'), referred to sixty-four years earlier by the Provençal gentleman Olivier de Serres in his *Théatre d'Agriculture, et Mesnage des Champs* (1600). De Serres enthusiastically praised the walnut for its all-round household usefulness, as a provider of oil and food throughout the year; and his country estate at Pradel, near Montélimar, now an agricultural college, still possesses a grand walnut avenue leading up to the front of the house.

In England walnut trees are found in parks and old gardens, and occasionally in churchyards, fields, and hedges. They never occur, however, in formal, public avenues, or in orchards as in south-eastern and south-western France; and it is rare to find a country house with a walnut avenue, except one created in conscious evocation of the past. A short-lived fashion for walnut groves in the gardens of Oxford colleges died out before the end of the eighteenth century, perhaps because the timber of the mature trees was in such high demand for furniture. Evelyn must have been aware of some form of the rustic, doggerel rhyme,

> A woman, a steak, and a walnut-tree,
> The more you beat 'em, the better they be

(referring either to beating the tree when the sap is rising, or to cudgelling down green walnuts in summer for pickles and preserves), since he remarked, rather frostily, 'In *Italy* they arm the Tops of long *Poles* with *Nails* and *Iron* for the purpose, and believe the *beating* improves the *Tree*; which I no more believe, than I do that Discipline would reform a Perverse *Shrew*.'

For the use of walnuts in *pâtisserie* and sweet dishes the best source of inspiration is central and eastern Europe, where, along the walnut-tree lined roads of Germany, Czechoslovakia, and the Great Hungarian Plain, the cult of the walnut developed into a serious form of self-indulgence. From Viennese *Nusscreme Torte* to Hungarian walnut slices, strudels, pancakes, and loaves or crescents (these last, according to George Lang's *Cuisine of Hungary*, specialities of Poszony, now Bratislava, capital of the Slovak Republic), the same enjoyment of walnuts is evident as an aspect of high gastronomic art. In south-eastern Europe, walnuts feature more simply in the various versions of festive *halva*: not the solidly confectioned blocks of ground sesame seeds, sugar, and honey on sale in English health-food and delicatessen shops, but a sweetened, moistened semolina dish, half cake, half pudding, containing walnuts, butter, sugar syrup, and (in some forms) milk and/or eggs.

Wet Walnuts

I've brought home some French wet walnuts from my local market. It's late October (the clocks go back this weekend) and walnuts have been in the shops for some weeks. On a walnut tree growing in a garden near here, the leaves have shrivelled and turned papery brown in an unexpected frost. Soon the trunk and bare branches will have their familiar appearance of ghostly grey lightness: a sight which can be seen between November and April in walnut orchards in south-eastern and south-western France, in parts of Italy and Spain, in central and south-eastern Europe, and eastwards through the Caucasus to Afghanistan and China. Here in England, walnut trees usually appear singly, and the nuts are rarely, if ever, harvested commercially. I look for them especially in parts of Somerset and Wiltshire, on limestone soil and in high, dry, sheltered places. There is a fine one in the churchyard at Isle Abbots, near Taunton; and the novelist John Cowper Powys, a clergyman's son, remembered the autumnal hampers which his parents would send him at boarding school from their parsonage at Montacute, full of 'walnuts from the tree in our field' and apples from the orchard. Walnuts used to be especially prized in England for ketchup, into which they were made while still unripe; and any over would be kept for dessert well into the New Year.

These wet walnuts are sweet and succulent. In the shell, some darker brown ones still feel slightly damp to the touch. When you break them open (the French have a special word, *cerneaux*, for wet walnuts, from the nut-pick used to prize them out of the shells), their skins are golden-brown or light bronze, and the nuts a new-parchment shade of white. They are proverbially good with new wine, and also with bread, cheese, and apples or celery for a simple autumn lunch.

Here is my favourite October lunch for a bright, chilly early afternoon. Several slices of home-made, wholemeal or granary bread, either with or without butter. A hunk of a mellow English or Welsh farmhouse Cheddar cheese. A small heap of wet walnuts, newly shelled. Several large leaves of basil (the fresh, strong taste of which goes very well with new walnuts); and large Italian white grapes, or a ripe Cox's Orange apple.

Chicken, Walnut, and Fresh Coriander Soup

I F YOU LIKE the mysterious, lingering taste of fresh coriander, you could enjoy this (to me) delectable autumn soup. The best kind of stock to make it with is a generously flavoured one, derived from the back, wings, and other spare parts of an uncooked chicken from which you used only the breasts and thighs for a previous meal. When making the stock, include a large juicy cut-up onion and plenty of black peppercorns.

SERVES 4

850 ml/1½ pints good strong chicken stock
90 g/3 oz fresh coriander
60 g/2 oz good wholemeal or other bread, crumbled
120 g/4 oz (shelled weight) fresh new walnuts, *or* mixed new
    walnuts and cashews
sea salt to taste

Strain and cool the stock, then place it in the refrigerator for several hours. Wash the coriander, cut off and discard the bottom inch of the stalks and any wilted leaves, and place the remainder on a board with the bread. Using a sharp knife, chop the coriander and bread together until the coriander juice permeates the bread. Grind the nuts together in a blender and add these to the bread and herb mixture. If necessary, cover and leave these ingredients for several hours.

When the stock has formed a skin of fat on the top, skim this off and heat up the stock in a large heavy pan. Add the bread, coriander, and nuts. (The walnuts must be fresh, juicy, newly shelled ones; hence the autumnal character of the soup.) Season with a teaspoon of sea salt if the stock was previously unsalted;

otherwise, add sea salt in moderation to taste. Bring the soup to the boil, then simmer for 5–10 minutes, turn off the heat, and allow to stand for up to half an hour before liquidizing. Reheat if necessary before serving.

Walnut Salad

THE VERY BEST new walnuts, with their fresh, mealy juices tasting like oats or wheat picked and chewed directly from the stem, need only a little sea salt and the sharpness of lemon juice to bring out their sweetness. Sadly, those which we buy ready-shelled in packets have often travelled thousands of miles and lain for months in store. With age they become bitter-tasting and flabby, then withered, hard, and dried out. If in any doubt about the age or palatability of your walnuts, make them into something sweet and cooked such as cakes or biscuits. But if they are firm and fresh-tasting, this salad can be a lovely appetizer or an accompaniment to Middle Eastern food or to a chicken or vegetable curry.

SERVES 2

120 g/4 oz wet or fresh-tasting shelled walnuts
2 tablespoons very finely chopped onion
½ teaspoon sea salt
juice of ½ lemon
2 tablespoons Greek-style yoghurt

Break up the walnuts as small as you can into a bowl. Add the onion, sea salt, lemon juice, and yoghurt, and mix well. The yoghurt should not curdle but should form a thin sauce when added to the other ingredients. Eat promptly, accompanied preferably by another small bowl of cucumber and yoghurt *raita*.

Walnut and Red Onion Confit Tart

A PLEASANT WINTER supper dish to serve, warm, on its own with broccoli or a salad, or with cold meat, game, or good Stilton. Shiny red onions make the best confit, a natural partner of cheese, walnuts, and savoury peppery pastry, to be enjoyed in generous quantities in this mildly sweet-sour tart.

SERVES 4

For the confit
570 g/1¼ lb red onions, peeled and thinly sliced
2 tablespoons sunflower oil
2 teaspoons brown sugar
sea salt
freshly ground black pepper
juice of ½ a lemon *or* 3–4 tablespoons red wine

For the pastry
120 g/4 oz strong white flour
60 g/2 oz wholemeal flour
freshly ground black pepper
90 g/3 oz butter
45 g/1½ oz Cheddar, grated (optional)
1–2 tablespoons cold water

For the filling

100 g/3½ oz (shelled weight) walnuts, broken into pieces

1 Cox's Orange or similar apple, peeled, cored, and thinly
  sliced

3–4 tablespoons single cream or top of the milk, *or* 60 g/2 oz
  Cheddar, grated

Halve the onion rings, which should be almost paper-thin. Heat
the oil over a moderate heat in a heavy frying pan, stir in the
onions, cover, and cook gently, stirring occasionally, for 20–30
minutes. By the end of this time the onions should have almost
caramelized. Stir in the brown, gooey deposit which they will have
begun to form on the bottom of the pan, and season with the sugar,
sea salt, freshly ground black pepper, and lemon juice or wine.
Continue simmering uncovered over a low heat while you prepare
the pastry.

Pre-heat the oven to 200°C/400°F, Gas mark 6. Combine the
two flours in a bowl, season with freshly ground black pepper, rub
in the butter until the mixture has the consistency of fine breadcrumbs, mix in the cheese if you wish, then bind with a very little
cold water until it forms a ball. Roll it out thinly and line an oiled,
22-cm/9-in flan dish. Bake the pastry blind for 5–10 minutes, then
cover it with the walnuts and apple slices and spoon on the confit.
Bake for 25–30 minutes, lowering the heat of the oven to 190°C/
375°F, Gas mark 5, after 10 minutes. Remove the tart from the
oven, make a hole in the centre of the filling, pour in the cream or
milk, and return to the oven for five minutes longer, or sprinkle the
top with grated Cheddar cheese and return to a cooling oven until
the cheese has just melted. Serve warm or at room temperature.

Walnut, Roquefort, and Tomato Tart

I USUALLY DISLIKE mixing nuts with tomatoes, since the sweetness of one seems to bear no relation to the acidity of the other. In this autumn tart, however, I have combined them, with Roquefort or a similar blue cheese (for example, Bleu des Causses, matured in the same limestone caverns as Roquefort) as the mediator between the two. The fully flavoured autumnal tomatoes from Spain or the Canaries are often sweeter than those available at other times; and the ambiguously sweet-sharp flesh of newly shelled wet walnuts invites a combination with other sweetish-sour or savoury tastes to bring out its sappy, woody-tasting character.

SERVES 3

60–75 g/2–2½ oz butter (see method)
30 g/1 oz Cheddar or Parmesan, grated
150 g/5 oz strong white flour
freshly ground black pepper
1–2 tablespoons cold water
2 tablespoons olive oil
450 g/1 lb well-flavoured tomatoes, skinned and thickly sliced
2–3 large cloves garlic, peeled and sliced
sea salt
60 g/2 oz (shelled weight) new walnuts, halved
120 g/4 oz Roquefort or other semi-soft blue ewe's milk cheese

Preheat the oven to 200°C/400°F, Gas mark 6. Rub the butter and grated cheese into the flour; if using Parmesan, increase the amount of butter to 75 g/2½ oz. Season with freshly ground black pepper. Add the water, a little at a time, until the pastry forms a ball, then roll this out on a floured board and use it to line a 22-cm/9-in flan dish or tin. Bake blind for 10 minutes until the pastry base begins to be crisp and brown.

Meanwhile heat 1 tablespoon of the oil in a medium-sized frying pan, add half the garlic, and soften it for a minute or two before adding half the tomato slices, taking care not to break these up. Season the tomato slices with sea salt and freshly ground black pepper, but do not turn them. Scatter the walnuts over the pastry base, interspersing them with half the blue cheese broken into small pieces. Put the tart into the oven for a minute or two until the cheese has begun to melt, then cover this with the tomato slices and garlic from the pan. Scatter the top with the remaining cheese and return the tart to the oven while you heat through the rest of the garlic and seasoned sliced tomatoes in another tablespoon of olive oil. When the second scattering of cheese has begun to melt, cover this with the rest of the tomato slices and garlic and return the tart to the oven for 20 minutes. Serve warm with a green salad as a light supper for an autumn evening.

Walnut and Mushroom Tartlets

THESE CRISP little tarts contain several different contrasting flavours and textures: light, cheesy pastry, clean-tasting walnuts, and the soft, slightly chewy mushrooms in their sauce. They are delicious simply eaten warm from the oven, and would make good party food – nourishing, savoury but not over-salted – to accompany a large plate of *crudités* with drinks. I like them at any time, however: as a portable light lunch dish, or a casual snack in mid-afternoon with a cup of strong Earl Grey.

MAKES 16–18 TARTLETS

For the pastry
60 g/2 oz butter
120 g/4 oz strong white flour
15 g/½ oz freshly grated Parmesan
2 egg yolks
freshly ground black pepper
2–3 tablespoons cold water

For the filling
1½ tablespoons sunflower oil
175 g/6 oz mushrooms, cleaned and finely sliced
30 g/1 oz butter
30 g/1 oz flour
6–8 tablespoons milk
15 g/½ oz freshly grated Parmesan
freshly grated nutmeg
2 egg whites
1 teaspoon *shoyu* or *tamari* (Japanese-style soy sauce)
60 g/2 oz (shelled weight) walnut halves or pieces

To make the pastry, rub the butter into the flour, add the Parmesan and work in the beaten egg yolks. Season with a little freshly ground black pepper, make a well in the centre, and add the water a tablespoon at a time until the pastry is just damp enough to form a consistent ball. Set this on one side to rest until you have made the filling, and preheat the oven to 200°C/400°F, Gas mark 6.

Heat the oil in a small heavy pan and add the mushrooms. Stir to coat with oil, cover, turn down the heat to medium/low and stew until the mushrooms have given off their juice.

In another, similar pan melt the butter over a medium/low heat and stir in the flour to form a *roux*. Add the mushroom liquid, continuing to stir, and then, spoon by spoon, as much of the milk as you need to form a fairly thick sauce. Turn off the heat, add the remaining Parmesan to the sauce, and season it with a little freshly grated nutmeg.

Season the mushrooms with the *shoyu* or *tamari*. (Parmesan *and* soy sauce? Yes; both seasonings are in such small quantities that they do not noticeably clash; and most available mushrooms need soy sauce to give them a savoury taste.) Roll out the pastry, cut it into circles about 7.5 cm/3 in in diameter and arrange in greased tartlet tins. Break up the walnut halves and place several small pieces in each pastry case. Cover with the mushroom slices. Whisk the egg whites until stiff, fold them into the sauce, and spoon this out into the tartlets, covering the mushrooms. Bake for 20 minutes until puffed up and golden.

Leek, Bacon, and Walnut Sauce with Tagliatelle

THIS CRUNCHY, protein-filled sauce makes a dish of tagliatelle into a satisfying main course.

SERVES 3

200 g/7 oz leeks, trimmed, washed, and very finely chopped
1 onion, peeled and finely chopped
3 tablespoons olive, walnut, or hazelnut oil
3 rashers unsmoked, thinly sliced back bacon, cut into 2-cm/
    1-in lengths
60 g/2 oz (shelled weight) walnuts, broken into small pieces
150 g/5 oz curd cheese

½ teaspoon sea salt
freshly ground black pepper
250 g/9 oz fresh tagliatelle
freshly grated Parmesan

Split the leeks lengthways, in half, and then (if fat ones) in half again, to achieve the right degree of fineness when you chop them. Rinse out any grit which may be lurking between the layers, then shave them crossways into a fine white and green mass.

Soften the onion and leeks for 15–20 minutes in 2 tablespoons of oil in a heavy covered pan. Fry the bacon separately in the remaining oil until lightly browned. Combine the onion, leeks, bacon, walnuts, and curd cheese and stir together thoroughly for a few minutes over a low heat until the cheese has heated through.

Boil the tagliatelle as directed with a pinch of sea salt, drain, season, and serve with the sauce, plenty of freshly grated Parmesan, and a plain green salad of lettuce (mixed with rocket if you have it) dressed with a little salt and olive or hazelnut oil.

Walnut Cheese Cream

A VERY SIMPLE and good recipe for a stiff mound of walnut cheese cream, perfect as an accompaniment to baked potatoes.

SERVES 3–4

60 g/2 oz cream cheese
60 g/2 oz mature Cheddar
120 g/4 oz walnut pieces
4 tablespoons *crème fraîche*

sea salt
freshly ground black pepper

Turn out the cream cheese into a bowl. (A slightly sharp cream cheese, of the sort obtainable at delicatessen counters, is the best kind to use for this.) Grate in the Cheddar, add the walnuts, stir in the *crème fraîche*, and season with a small pinch of sea salt and a couple of grinds of black pepper. Pound the mixture with the tip of a spoon until the walnut pieces have broken up small enough to blend with the creamy cheese, then heap it up on a plate and serve.

Lamb with Apricots, Spinach, and Walnuts

THIS IS A deliciously light, well-balanced dish with many Middle Eastern precedents. Lamb with apricots, lamb with nuts (pistachio or walnut), and lamb with spinach all belong to a pattern of cooking which extends, with regional variations, from the southern and eastern Mediterranean through Iran to Afghanistan and the borders of north-western India. In this dish the four main ingredients balance one another: the apricots providing a sweetish acidity which blends well with the exquisitely flavoured juices of the lamb, the spinach giving softness, and the walnuts crunch.

SERVES 4

3 tablespoons sunflower oil
1 large onion, peeled and chopped

450 g/1 lb boneless lean leg of lamb, cubed
seeds from 10–12 cardamom pods
3 large cloves garlic, peeled and chopped
sea salt
125 g/4 oz dried apricots, pre-soaked and chopped
400 g/14 oz spinach, washed and trimmed
225 g/8 oz basmati rice + 570 ml/1 pint water
90 g/3 oz shelled walnuts, broken
4–5 tablespoons water

Heat half the oil in a heavy casserole, add the onion, cover, and soften over a low to moderate heat for 10 minutes. Heat the remaining oil in a frying pan and brown the cubes of lamb in it, stirring continuously for 3–4 minutes over a high heat. Add the lamb to the onion, cover the casserole, and leave over a very low heat while you crush the cardamom seeds, first alone in a mortar and then with the garlic and a pinch of sea salt. The combined scents of cardamom and garlic, unmixed with any other spice, can be exhilaratingly sharp and almost lemony, like citronella oil. Stir the cardamom and garlic into the lamb, add the apricots, cover the casserole again, and place in a gentle oven, 170°C/325°F, Gas mark 3, for half an hour. The lamb gives off its own juices which infuse the apricots, and need diluting with water only towards the end of cooking.

Place the spinach in a saucepan with the water which clings to the leaves from the last washing and half a teaspoon of sea salt. Bring to the boil and cook over a high heat for 2–3 minutes. Put the rice on to boil with just under twice its volume of water and another half-teaspoon of sea salt. (This should be ready after 15 minutes' simmering, inclusive of the time taken to bring it to the boil.) Drain the spinach, press out the rough-tasting liquid, chop it on a plate, and add it to the lamb stew with the walnut pieces and a few tablespoons of water. Cover the pieces of lamb with spinach and press this well down so that it absorbs the casserole juices. Return the casserole to the oven until the rice is ready, then serve with a mound of rice on each plate and a generous helping of the lamb stew over it.

Roast Chicken with Celery and Walnut Sauce

C HICKEN WITH a stuffing or sauce of walnuts is a gastronomic combination especially characteristic of the mountainous walnut-growing countries in the extreme south of the former USSR. Circassian chicken, a classic Caucasian dish, consists of slices of hot cooked chicken served on a bed of rice and covered with a sauce of crushed walnuts lubricated with stock and decorated with a dribble of red-coloured oil. (This is the form in which the recipe appears in Claudia Roden's comprehensive *Book of Middle Eastern Food*.) Variations on this dish exist in the traditional cooking of Georgia, where walnuts are used regularly in cooking. In this recipe I have given the dish a more English slant by combining the walnuts with chopped cooked celery, so that the sauce doubles as a vegetable dish. It makes an interesting substitute, in both flavour and texture, for bread sauce when serving a conventionally cooked English-style roast chicken with roast potatoes, a green vegetable such as spinach or cauliflower, and gravy.

SERVES 4–5

1 1.5 kg/3 lb roasting chicken (preferably free-range), stuffed (see method)

5 large sticks well-flavoured green celery (or 7–8 smaller
   ones), washed
2 tablespoons sunflower oil
5 large cloves garlic, peeled
75 g/2½ oz (shelled weight) newly shelled walnuts, broken
   into pieces
150 ml/5 fl oz vegetable water or stock
½ teaspoon sea salt
freshly ground black pepper
pan juices from the chicken

Put on the chicken to roast with a stuffing of bread, butter, and a crushed clove of garlic (or any alternative stuffing other than a nut one). Allowing half an hour for the celery to cook, chop it as finely as you can and put it with the sunflower oil in a small heavy covered pan over a low heat. Shake occasionally, but avoid removing the lid. The celery should eventually cook in its own steam with the least possible loss of flavour.

Place the garlic cloves under or near the chicken to roast. Crush the walnuts in a bowl, ideally with a wooden pestle, so that they become coarsely mealy (but not as oily as they would become if crushed even for a very short time in an electric blender). As you do so, add a little liquid, such as stock or the water from parboiling potatoes, for lubrication. When the garlic has softened and begun to turn golden, crush this into the walnuts. Gradually add the softened celery and its liquid and crush this into the walnut and garlic mixture with the pestle. Add some pan juices from the roasting chicken and more stock or potato-water. Season with the sea salt and some freshly ground black pepper and return the finished sauce to the celery pan to keep warm until the chicken is ready to carve. When serving, treat as a purée to be served beside, rather than under or over, the chicken.

Potatoes with Walnut and Cheese Sauce

A PERUVIAN recipe from Alberto Portugheis, concert pianist, gourmet, Latin American restaurateur, and chef.

SERVES 4 AS A MAIN COURSE OR 8 AS A STARTER

4 dried chillies, de-seeded
1 onion, peeled and sliced
75 ml/3 fl oz peanut oil
2 cloves garlic, peeled and finely chopped
120 g/4 oz (shelled weight) walnuts
120 g/4 oz crumbly cheese (e.g. Lancashire, Caerphilly, Cheshire)
300 ml/10 fl oz milk
sea salt
freshly ground black pepper
4 large potatoes
1 round lettuce
4 hard-boiled eggs, shelled and halved lengthwise
8 black olives
1 red pepper, de-seeded, fried or grilled and cut in strips

Soak the chillies in hot water for half an hour, then drain them. Soften the onion in the oil for 15–20 minutes until pale golden, then add the garlic and cook for another 20 seconds. Add the chillies, walnuts, and crumbled cheese, and blend everything together in a liquidizer or food processor. Gradually dilute this purée with milk in a saucepan over a gentle heat until it forms a thickish white sauce, and season it with sea salt and freshly ground black pepper.

By now the potatoes, boiled in their skins Portuguese-style, should be cooked and drained. Peel them and place them cut-side downwards on a bed of lettuce leaves in a dish. Cover the potatoes with the sauce and decorate them with the white and yellow hard-boiled eggs, the black olives, and the red pepper, surrounding the dish with vivid green shredded lettuce. The combination of potatoes, red pepper, cheese, and nuts is particularly nourishing and vitamin-rich.

Walnut Filo Pie

FILO PASTRY can be overrated as a container for anything and everything; but it makes a good light basis for a covered tart filled with confectioner's custard and nuts. This flattish crisp pie is cut into squares or oblongs, and is best eaten very fresh, still slightly warm or just cooled, as a tea-time cake or dessert.

SERVES 5–6

4–5 sheets fresh or thawed filo pastry
300 ml/10 fl oz milk
½ vanilla pod, slit lengthways
75 g/2½ oz Demerara or golden granulated sugar
4–5 egg yolks
120 g/4 oz Ricotta or curd cheese
120 g/4 oz (shelled weight) walnuts broken into pieces

Line an oiled 30 × 25-cm/12 × 10-in baking-sheet with two thicknesses of filo pastry, allowing a little of the filo to overlap the edges. Heat the milk to boiling point in a heavy-bottomed pan, add the vanilla pod and sugar, lower the heat, and whisk in the egg yolks one by one. Continue stirring over a gentle heat with a wooden spoon, making sure that the custard does not stick to the bottom of the pan, until the custard is thick, smooth, and strongly vanilla-flavoured. To ensure that you get the maximum flavour out of the vanilla pod, scrape out the tiny black seeds which fill the interior and transfer these into the custard.

Set the oven to 190°C/375°F, Gas mark 5. Remove the vanilla pod and discard it or wash it for re-use. (If you have scraped out the seeds, it will now give only a faint flavour of vanilla.) Put the custard into a blender with the Ricotta or curd cheese and blend until smooth. Scatter the walnut pieces over the pastry, pour the custard over them, and turn in the overhanging edges of the filo to enclose it. Cover with a single sheet of filo, and bake for 20 minutes or until the top is lightly brown. Cool on a rack.

Walnut and Ginger Parcels

B OTH WALNUTS and preserved ginger in syrup are exported in large quantities from China, a fact which underlines the affinity of these two delicious foods with one another. These little parcels are a nourishing snack or dessert, eaten plain, with an apple or banana, or as an accompaniment to plain Greek-style yoghurt with a dash of ginger juice and honey (imported from Malaysia and sold at Culpeper's herbalists' shops in London and elsewhere in Britain).

As Western medicine has drawn closer to Chinese herbal medicine and to the Ayurvedic remedies traditionally used in India, ginger, with its instantly warming effect, has become acknowledged in the West to be a major health-food. It is effective against arthritis and rheumatism and helps the heart by protecting polyunsaturated fats against peroxidative attack. Walnuts, too, have been found to be good for the heart in lowering blood cholesterol levels. In combination, therefore, ginger and walnuts should be in every diet for a long life.

MAKES ABOUT 15 PARCELS

For the pastry
60 g/2 oz butter
120 g/4 oz strong white flour
1 tablespoon cold water

For the filling
5 pieces preserved ginger
120 g/4 oz (shelled weight) walnut halves
2 tablespoons Greek-style yoghurt
2 tablespoons syrup from ginger

Make the pastry by rubbing the butter into the flour and adding just enough water to form a consistent ball. Roll this out thinly and divide it into triangles, circles, or oblongs: whatever shape suits you best for forming into little parcels.

Remove the pieces of ginger from their syrup and chop each one into 20–25 small chunks. Lightly grind some of the walnuts (about half will do) in a blender, taking care not to over-grind them into an oily pulp. Empty the ground walnuts into a bowl, break up the rest of the walnuts into smallish pieces, and add these for contrast. Stir in the yoghurt and ginger syrup, then the ginger pieces. The filling will now have an exhilaratingly tingling, nutty taste and a chunky, semi-liquid texture. Spoon about a teaspoonful of this on to each segment of pastry, gather up the sides and seal the edges together. Pre-heat the oven to 200°C/400°F, Gas mark 6, and bake the parcels on an oiled baking-tray for 15–20 minutes until golden.

Mascarpone with Ginger and Walnuts

M ASCARPONE is a soft, rich, Italian cows' milk cheese made from ripened pasteurized cream. It is lighter and smoother in texture than *crème fraîche*, with a slightly blander flavour, and can be used as a longer-lasting, more digestible substitute for fresh thick cream. It is the most suitable kind of cream cheese to eat with walnuts as a dessert, and (like fresh cream) is also delicious mixed with ginger syrup.

In England, one can now buy bottles of Malaysian ginger juice with honey from Culpeper shops. I still, however, enjoy making my own ginger syrup, the only necessary equipment for which, apart from saucepan and wooden spoon, is a small-size *moulin-légumes* of the kind sold for straining baby-food.

SERVES 6

4–5 tablespoons ginger syrup (see separate recipe below)
500 g/1 lb 2 oz Mascarpone
2 tablespoons thick honey
150 g/5 oz (shelled weight) freshly shelled walnuts, broken
    into pieces

Make the ginger syrup as directed. Empty the Mascarpone into a large bowl with the honey and walnut pieces and beat together until soft. Add the syrup a little at a time, beating it in, until you have the desired strength of taste. Serve for dessert with fine thin wafers or walnut biscuits.

Ginger Syrup

45 g/1½ oz fresh ginger root, peeled and cut into small cubes
100 g/3½ oz Demerara sugar
300 ml/10 fl oz water

Place the ginger root and sugar in a small heavy-bottomed saucepan and pound them together with a wooden spoon until the ginger juice begins to soak into the sugar. Add the water, bring to the boil, and simmer for 20–25 minutes, topping up the water if the syrup seems in danger of reducing to a thick, sticky toffee. The liquid should eventually reduce by nearly two-thirds. Put the syrup through the *moulin-légumes* (not an electric liquidizer, since this will not eliminate the fibres) and scrape carefully to incorporate all the sieved ginger into the syrup. If not used at once, this syrup will store well in a screw-topped jar in the fridge.

Chocolate Walnut Tart

A TRULY DELICIOUS, rich-tasting, simple tart, which repays buying a strong, Continental-style plain chocolate. Some supermarkets (e.g. Waitrose) stock excellent own brands.

SERVES 4–6

For the pastry
150 g/5 oz strong white flour
75 g/2½ oz butter
1–2 tablespoons cold water

For the filling
45 g/1½ oz unsalted butter
90 g/3 oz Demerara sugar
9 tablespoons milk
90 g/3 oz plain chocolate (preferably 70% cocoa solids),
    broken into pieces
3 eggs, separated
90 g/3 oz (shelled weight) walnut pieces

Make the pastry, rubbing the cut-up butter into the flour and adding just enough water to make a consistent ball. Set the oven to 200°C/400°F, Gas mark 6. Roll the pastry out thinly, line an oiled 25-cm/10-in flan dish with it, and bake it blind for 10–15 minutes until it has begun to set but is not yet brown.

Melt the unsalted butter in a small heavy-bottomed saucepan. Stir in the sugar, then add the milk and boil it up until you have a foaming, butterscotch liquid. Add the chocolate, and when this has melted remove from the heat and beat in the egg yolks. Scatter the walnut pieces over the pastry. Whip the egg whites until stiff, fold these into the chocolate mixture, then pour this over the walnuts. Lower the oven temperature to 190°C/375°F, Gas mark 5, and bake the tart for another 25 minutes until the filling is risen and set. Serve cold.

Chocolate, Coffee, and Walnut Cream

A RICH, sophisticated and simple dessert, with complementary
flavours which will develop as it stands and cools, and
which improve with keeping. Allow time when making it for the
chocolate/coffee/walnut mixture to become completely cold before
you stir in the whipped cream, or the eventual consistency will be
too runny.

SERVES 6

100 g/3½ oz plain chocolate (ideally 70% cocoa solids)
250 ml/8 fl oz milk
60 g/2 oz Demerara sugar
250 ml/8 fl oz strong black coffee
2 egg yolks + 1 whole egg, beaten together
120 g/4 oz walnut halves or pieces, lightly ground or crushed
250 ml/8 fl oz whipping cream

Break up the chocolate into a heavy-bottomed saucepan and melt
it into the milk. It greatly improves the flavour of this dish to use
the newly popular bitter chocolate made with 70% cocoa solids;
this also has the advantage of setting well after melting. Add the
sugar, then the coffee, and quickly raise the temperature to just
below boiling-point. Stir in the beaten eggs with a wooden spoon
and immediately lower the temperature to simmering-point, continuing to stir until the mixture has thickened. Remove from the
heat and fold in walnuts. (If these have oiled from over-grinding,
you may need to add them in a blender to eliminate lumps.) Pour
out into a pudding-basin or bowl and leave to stand in a cool place
until completely cold and thick. Then, and only then, whip the

cream and fold it into the custard before serving. This is good with very plain un-sweet biscuits, for example Cornish Wafers. The rough-textured ground walnuts give a pleasant unevenness to this interesting dessert, while their slight bitterness echoes that of the chocolate and the black coffee.

Apple, Ginger, and Walnut Pudding

WALNUTS, ginger, and apples all go well together; and a ginger syrup brings a stimulating, sparkling taste to fluffy Bramley cooking apples. This is a light, digestible, yet nourishing pudding, good for using up spare egg whites, if (for example) you have recently made the rich Chestnut, Chocolate, and Coffee Cream pudding on page 95.

SERVES 4

45 g/1½ oz fresh ginger root, peeled and chopped
120 g/4 oz Demerara *or* golden granulated sugar
250 ml/8 fl oz water
450 g/1 lb ripe Bramley apples, peeled, cored, and sliced
175 g/6 oz (shelled weight) walnuts
3 egg whites, whisked until stiff

Place the ginger and sugar in a small heavy-bottomed saucepan and pound them together with the tip of a wooden spoon until the sugar is saturated in ginger juice. Cover with the water, bring to the boil, and simmer gently for 20–25 minutes until you have a powerful-tasting ginger syrup.

Put the apples in a saucepan and strain the syrup over them, or (ideally) push it through a small hand food-mill (*moulin-légumes*), of the kind which you can buy for sieving babies' food. This enables you to use as much as possible of the aromatic ginger pulp, while excluding the fibrous parts of the ginger. Cover the pan and cook the apples and syrup over a moderate heat for about 10 minutes until the apples have softened to a purée. Pre-heat the oven to 200°C/400°F, Gas mark 6.

Lightly grind the walnuts and stir them into the apple purée, then fold in the egg whites. Bake the pudding in a buttered, oven-proof dish for about 20 minutes, or until lightly browned on top, and serve warm or at room temperature.

Butterscotch Pears and Walnuts with Greek Yoghurt

THIS QUICK and simple pudding, with its spicy butterscotch sauce, can transform the dull, mass-produced pears which are so often to be found in supermarkets.

SERVES 4

45 g/1½ oz butter
90 g/3 oz Demerara sugar
½ teaspoon cinnamon
150 ml/5 fl oz milk
4 large, firm pears (e.g. Conference), peeled, cored, and sliced
    vertically into eighths

12–15 walnuts (shelled weight), freshly shelled and halved or
broken
225 g/8 oz Greek-style yoghurt

Melt the butter in a heavy-bottomed saucepan over a moderate heat,
but do not let it go brown. Stir in the sugar and cinnamon, continue
stirring for half a minute, then add the milk and bring to a foaming
boil. Stir thoroughly again for 1–2 minutes while the butterscotch
sauce boils and reduces, then stir in the sliced pears, reduce the heat
to just above simmering point, and poach the pears in the sauce,
uncovered, for 5–10 minutes. By this time the pears will have given
off some of their juice to flavour the sauce. Add the walnuts (recently
shelled ones are best) and turn out into a dish to cool.

Serve at room temperature, topping each helping with a
generous dollop of Greek yoghurt.

Banana and Walnut Cake

B ANANA CAKE should be superlatively light: hence the high
proportion of egg whites to yolks in this recipe. I am not a
great devotee of banana cakes in general; but this one, containing
walnuts, has a degree of taste and crunch which rescues it from
insipidity.

SERVES 4–6

---

150 g/5 oz strong white flour
1 teaspoon baking powder
75 g/2½ oz butter

225 g/8 oz (peeled weight) bananas
90 g/3 oz (shelled weight) walnuts, broken into pieces
90 g/3 oz Demerara or soft brown sugar
zest of 1 lemon
1 egg yolk
3 egg whites

Pre-heat the oven to 190°C/375°F, Gas mark 5. Mix the flour with the baking powder in a mixing-bowl. Rub in the butter until the flour has the consistency of fine breadcrumbs; then do the same with the bananas. Stir in the walnut pieces, sugar, lemon zest, and egg yolk. The mixture should by now be quite loose and wet. Whisk the egg whites in a separate bowl until they form peaks, then fold in the banana mixture. Line a loaf-shaped tin with oiled and floured baking-parchment, spoon in the cake mixture, and bake for 35–40 minutes, or until a fork inserted into the centre of the cake comes out clean.

Coffee Semolina Cake with Walnut Filling

I FIRST MADE this cake with a cashew nut filling, then decided that walnuts, with their dark, oily character, were perfect in combination with the other ingredients. The cake has an oriental feeling (if less sweet than most Middle Eastern cakes and pastries), and is a wonderfully sustaining snack at any time of the day.

Semolina is a flinty wheat-grain from the type of hard wheat which, when milled, makes the super-strong flour suitable for pasta, and has long been highly regarded for its nourishing properties and usefulness as a basis for special desserts all over Eastern Europe and the Middle East. In India, semolina makes *ladoo*, solidly satisfying, rough-textured sweets with a flavouring of cardamom. In Near Eastern countries, and in parts of south-eastern Europe where oriental influences are strong, it is baked into moist desserts or cakes such as *halva*, which, like pastries, are further moistened after baking by soaking in a sweet syrup. In traditional Russian cooking, as *Gurevskaya kasha*, it makes a creamy pudding decorated and flavoured with cream, fruit, and nuts. All this is a long way from the dense, cloyingly textured white stodge of the English school puddings of my childhood, when only a spoonful of jam relieved the monotony of texture and taste of semolina which had been lumpily boiled.

Baking is undoubtedly the most interesting way of cooking semolina, provided that it is kept moist and enriched, since it dries out very easily in the oven. Much of the pleasure involved in making this cake is in combining the ingredients to keep it moist, including the filling, which, unusually, is baked in the cake.

SERVES 4–6

---

120 g/4 oz walnut pieces
2 tablespoons Greek-style yoghurt
1½ tablespoons honey or Demerara sugar
60 g/2 oz butter
90 g/3 oz Demerara sugar
8 tablespoons creamy milk
250 g/9 oz semolina
1 heaped teaspoon baking powder
6 tablespoons strong black coffee
icing sugar (optional)

Preheat the oven to 200°C/400°F, Gas mark 6. Grind up 90 g/3 oz of walnut pieces in a blender (taking care not to over-grind them, since walnuts become oily very soon), and mix them with the yoghurt and a tablespoon of honey or Demerara sugar. Set this filling on one side.

Melt the butter in a saucepan, stir in the sugar, and cook these together for a minute or two over a gentle heat. Measure in the milk and bring this to the boil so that you have a rich foaming butterscotch-flavoured liquid. Turn off the heat, allow the liquid to subside, then add the semolina, the baking powder, and the remaining walnut pieces, and beat until all the liquid has been absorbed. Add 4 tablespooons of coffee and beat again until you have a thick, fluffy batter.

Grease an 18½-cm/7½-in spring-clip sponge tin and pour in half the semolina mixture, spreading it with a spoon or wet hands until it forms an even layer. Spoon the filling over this, taking it as near as you can to the edge of the tin, and cover it with the rest of the semolina, smoothing this out to form a flat-topped cake. If a little of the filling escapes round the edge this will not be noticeable once the cake is cooked. Bake for about 20 minutes until the surface is nicely browned and covered in a network of cracks; then mix the remaining 2 tablespoons of coffee with the remaining half tablespoon honey and spoon this over the top of the cake as a syrup, allowing it to permeate the cracks and soak in round the edge of the upper layer. (If the semolina has become very dry, it may need an extra tablespoon of coffee.) Return the cake to the oven for a minute or two, then remove it and allow it to cool in the tin. Turn the cake out carefully straight on to a plate, since you will find it less cohesive than the kind made with flour and eggs. If you feel that the top needs decoration, dredge it with a little icing sugar.

Walnut and Ginger Layer Cake

A THOROUGHLY indulgent cake, filled with ginger-flavoured, Hungarian-inspired butter-cream, for the bleakest, most dispiriting days of winter.

SERVES 4–6

For the syrup
30 g/1 oz ginger root, peeled and chopped
90 g/3 oz Demerara or soft brown sugar
250 ml/8 fl oz water

For the cake
60 g/2 oz butter
75 g/2½ oz soft brown sugar
5 eggs, separated
120 g/4 oz flour
1 teaspoon baking powder
60 g/2 oz (shelled weight) walnuts
2–3 tablespoons syrup (as above)

For the filling
30 g/1 oz butter
30 g/1 oz soft brown sugar
2–3 tablespoons syrup (as above)
142 ml/5 fl oz carton double cream, whipped

Half an hour before mixing the cake (a basic sponge, enriched and made heavier with additions of walnuts and ginger syrup), prepare the ginger syrup, as in the recipe for Apple, Ginger, and Walnut Pudding (see page 186). Simmer this for 20–25 minutes, then pass it through a hand-operated food mill.

Pre-heat the oven to 200°C/400°F, Gas mark 6, and grease two sponge tins. Cream the butter and sugar together, add the egg yolks, and continue creaming with a knife-blade until the mixture is light. Gradually add the flour and baking powder, then the ginger syrup and walnuts. Fold in the stiffly beaten egg whites, turn out the mixture at once into the baking tins, smooth down the surface with a wet knife-blade, and bake for 15–18 minutes. When the cake is cooked so that a fork emerges from it cleanly, turn it out on to a rack to cool.

For the filling, cream together the butter and sugar, then add the ginger syrup. This gives you a very loose mixture, which will firm up later as the butter hardens again. Whisk the cream until very stiff, then stir in the ginger butter cream. Leave to cool for a little in the refrigerator, and spread generously over the lower half of the cake when this is quite cool. Smooth any remaining ginger syrup over the surface of the cake for a glaze.

Eliza Acton's Green Walnut Catsup

CATSUPS or ketchups, popularized by the eightheeth-century British in India, were in great demand in Eliza Acton's day in the 1840s, together with bottled sauces flavoured with anchovy essence, soy sauce, and spices. Their chief purpose was probably to make palatable the large quantities of cold meat which were eaten either for breakfast or, increasingly, for lunch. Walnut and mushroom were among the favourite ketchups.

100 green walnuts
225 g/8 oz salt

1.1 1/2 pints malt vinegar
1.1 1/2 pints strong beer
225 g/8 oz anchovy fillets
1 head large-cloved garlic
15 g/½ oz ground nutmeg
15 g/½ oz cloves, bruised
15 g/½ oz freshly ground black pepper
8 g/¼ oz mace

'Pound in a mortar a hundred young walnuts, strewing amongst them as they are done half a pound of salt; then pour to them a quart of strong vinegar, and let them stand until they have become quite black, keeping them stirred three or four times a day; next add a quart of strong old beer, and boil the whole together for 10 minutes; strain it, and let it remain until the next day; then pour it off clear from the sediment, add to it half a pound of anchovies, one large head of garlic bruised, half an ounce of nutmegs bruised, the same quantity of cloves and black pepper, and two drachms of mace: boil these together for half an hour, and the following day boil and cork the catsup well. It will keep for a dozen years. Many persons add to it, before it is boiled, a bottle of port wine; and others recommend a large bunch of sweet herbs to be put in with the spice.'

Modern Cookery . . . for Private Families (1845)

Claire Loewenfeld's Green Walnut Marmalade

FROM *Nuts* (1957). An excellent, if sweet, source of Vitamin C.

MAKES JUST OVER 450 G/1 LB

225 g/8 oz green walnuts
575 ml/1 pint boiling water
340 g/12 oz sugar
¾ teaspoon citric acid *or* juice of 1 lemon

Slice the walnuts into the boiling water and boil steadily for 40 minutes, then add the sugar and the citric acid or lemon juice and boil for a further 20 minutes until set. Pot in sterilized jars. For green walnut jam, sieve before adding the sugar, then boil again for 20–40 minutes.

BIBLIOGRAPHY

Acton, Eliza, *Modern Cookery . . . for Private Families* (1845). Abridged as *The Best of Eliza Acton*, selected and edited by Elizabeth Ray with an introduction by Elizabeth David (Longman, 1968)

Apicius, *Cookery and Dining in Imperial Rome: A Bibliography, Critical Review and Translation of the Ancient Book known as* Apicius de re Coquinaria, edited and translated by Joseph Dommers Vehling with an introduction by Prof. Frederick Starr (Dover, New York, 1977)

Atwood, Mary S., *Adventures in Indian Cooking* (Bombay, 1972)

Austin, Thomas (ed.), *Two Fifteenth-Century Cook Books: Harleian MS 279 (about 1430) and Harleian MS 4016 (about 1450)* . . . (Early English Texts Society 91, Oxford University Press, 1888)

Carper, Jean, *The Food Pharmacy Cookbook* (Simon and Schuster, 1991)

Carter, Elizabeth, *Majorcan Food and Cookery* (Prospect Books, 1989)

Castelvetro, Giacomo, *The Fruit, Herbs and Vegetables of Italy*, translated with an introduction by Gillian Riley (Viking, 1989)

Chamberlain, Lesley, *The Food and Cooking of Eastern Europe* (Penguin, 1989)

Cobbett, William, *Rural Rides* (1830; Penguin English Library, edited with an introduction by George Woodcock, 1967)

De Serres, Olivier, *Théatre d'Agriculture, et Mesnage des Champs* (1600)

Duke, J. A., *Handbook of Legumes of World Economic Importance* (Plenum, 1981)

Encyclopedia of Food Science, Food Technology and Nutrition (Academic Press, 1993)

Evelyn, John, *Sylva, or a Discourse of Forest-trees* (1664)

Francatelli, Charles Elmé, *The Royal Confectioner, English and Foreign* (1874)

Grigson, Jane, *Good Things* (Penguin, 1973)

Holland, B., Unwin, I. D., and Buss, D. H., *Fruit and Nuts. The first supplement to McCance and Widdowson's* The Composition of Foods, 5th edition (Royal Society of Chemistry, 1992)

Lang, George, *The Cuisine of Hungary* (Penguin, 1985)

Loewenfeld, Claire, *Nuts* (Faber and Faber, 1957)

Norman, Jill, *Nuts* (Dorling Kindersley, National Trust Little Library, 1990)

Ortiz, Elizabeth Lambert, *The Food of Spain and Portugal* (Headline, 1990)

Petrova, Nina, *Russian Cookery* (Penguin, 1968)

Pinińska, Mary, *The Polish Kitchen* (Macmillan, 1990)

Roden, Claudia, *A Book of Middle Eastern Food* (Penguin, 1970)

Spurling, Hilary, *Elinor Fettiplace's Receipt Book* (Penguin, 1987)

INDEX